FREES
COOK

COOKERY WITHOUT RECIPES

FREESTYLE COOKING

COOKERY WITHOUT RECIPES

Tony Freeman

RIGHT WAY

Typeset in 11/12pt Times by Letterpart Ltd., Reigate, Surrey.

Printed and bound in Great Britain by Cox & Wyman Ltd., Reading, Berkshire.

The *Right Way* series is published by Elliot Right Way Books, Brighton Road, Lower Kingswood, Tadworth, Surrey, KT20 6TD, U.K.

CONTENTS

DEDICATION

To Gill, who ate all my experiments (and gained weight).

1

INTRODUCTION – READ THIS FIRST

Who Is This Book For?
If you're the sort of person who reads the first few pages of a recipe book – you know, the interesting ones that talk about methods and ingredients and cooking – and then get bored when you get to the actual recipes, then this book's for you.

There are two categories of people in the world: those who put everybody into two categories and those who don't. I'm an unashamed categoriser and I know that there are people who like and use recipe books and those who don't. This book is aimed at people who want to cook but don't want to use recipes.

All cooking needs improvisation because, however slavishly you might try to follow a recipe, something in your kitchen will always be different from the kitchen where the recipe was worked out. A lot of people, and I'm one of them, rely almost entirely on improvisation and don't follow recipes at all, although I do use recipes to get ideas and to work out the basics of what is going on.

I've written this book for myself as I was when I started cooking. I looked at recipe books and found that they don't show you how to cook but just give a bunch of examples for you to copy. As part of my research for this book I looked in the cookery sections of several bookshops and I found that there are hundreds of books of recipes but none of them tell you how to cook.

Cookery books tend to make cooking look difficult because they make a point of saying how many different recipes there are (mostly to sell the books; who'd buy a cookery book with no recipes?). What I want to show is the similarities in cooking techniques, not the differences.

The idea of this book is to explain what cooking is about in enough detail for you to 'do your own thing'. It's up to you to choose whether or not you should use other people's recipes from now on.

Health And Sanity Warning

There's a good chance that when you start out what you cook won't come out as expected. It's most unlikely that a meal will be totally inedible but it's best to take some precautions:

1.   Have the phone number of your favourite Pizza delivery, Chippy or Kebab shop handy.
2.   Have something quick and easy standing by in a cupboard or in the freezer.
3.   Don't try something new at an important dinner party.

Why Bother?

If you're looking at this book then you've probably already decided that you want to cook for yourself but, if you're not sure, let's talk about some of the reasons why it's a good thing.

The alternative to cooking for yourself is to go out to restaurants all the time or to buy convenience foods and heat them up at home. There's nothing wrong with convenience food, some of my best friends eat it, but it is different from home cooking. Convenience food is more expensive than doing it all yourself.

Having the preparation, presentation and packaging done by someone else is costly so, if the convenience food is cheap, you can be fairly sure that poor quality ingredients have been used. If you buy the raw ingredients yourself you have better control over what you're eating. If you do all the preparation yourself you'll know exactly what went into what you eat. If you have allergies, or cook for someone who has, you can leave out the trigger foods and if you're worried about additives you can leave them out too.

Convenience foods need additives to preserve them and to ensure that their structure doesn't break down on storage. They also have to stand around for a while when being transported

2

YOUR LIFE IN MY HANDS

Now Read This

Even if you don't read any other part of this book read this: it might save your life!

Because of the nature of this book I feel a special responsibility for your safety but I can't stand behind you watching over your shoulder all the time so you're going to have to learn how to look after yourself. Most cookery books tell you what to do every step of the way so they can warn you about safety problems as they arise in the cooking procedure. I can't do that because I'm not giving you a cooking procedure. All I can do is to warn you about the hazards I know about and suggest what precautions you can take to deal with them. I can also suggest what you can do about any other hazards that I don't know about. You'll find some of this stuff repeated elsewhere in the book but safety is so important that I think some repetition is necessary.

Natural Born Killers

Some natural foodstuffs are poisonous in themselves unless they're prepared properly. The leaves of rhubarb are poisonous and should be thrown away. Potatoes that have started to turn green are poisonous and shouldn't be eaten. The bitter variety of cassava is poisonous until it's cooked. Red kidney beans are poisonous until they've been boiled, vigorously, for at least 15 minutes and they'll still need to be cooked for at least an hour to be edible. Some bits of some fishes are also poisonous. I'm sure I haven't listed everything so if you're unfamiliar with a new food don't be afraid to ask how to prepare it when you buy. In my experience people selling unusual foods are only too pleased to talk about them to a possible new customer.

Some natural foods can be confused with natural things that are definitely not food. Mushrooms and toadstools are closely related, and similar looking, fungi but while the mushrooms are excellent food the toadstools are extremely poisonous. It's the same with berries: many are good food and many are very poisonous. There are other examples, such as flowers, which you may want to experiment with and which may be poisonous. The only way to deal with this is either: to buy from reputable shops; or to make absolutely sure that you know what you're looking at if you collect from the wild. Remember that there are laws against picking wild plants and you should always get the permission of the owner of any land that you go onto, for whatever reason.

The pesticides and fertilisers used to grow vegetables can be toxic to humans so you should always wash fruit and vegetables before you eat them.

The Never Ending Battle

The thing you've really got to fight against in the kitchen is food poisoning. What we call spoilage is only nature recycling our food into the environment before we've had a chance to eat it ourselves. Unfortunately, the results of this recycling are often toxic to us. A whole lot of different bugs (mostly bacteria and fungi) cause spoilage. You probably know some of them by name, for example: Salmonella, Listeria, Clostridium Botulinum, Staphylococcus and Streptococcus. You can't keep up with all the names and all the possible sources of contamination but you don't have to. You just have to be suspicious of everything and treat it as if it might be contaminated.

Heat kills all the bugs so all you have to do is make sure that everything you eat has been cooked thoroughly. The bugs won't survive temperatures over 63°C so anything over that makes your food safe and sterile. You have to keep it at that temperature for several minutes to make sure that the food is heated through. If you want to eat anything raw or ready prepared then you have to trust that the supplier has either prevented any contamination or has done the heat treatment for you.

This is why there are so many food poisoning scares in the news these days. A couple of generations ago people bought fresh ingredients, prepared them themselves and didn't expect them to keep for long. Our expectations are different now. Because suppliers have been very good at providing us with safe wholesome food we now expect them to be perfect and so we assume that all our food is safe all the time. This has made us complacent and careless with food preparation and hygiene. So, when there is any contamination we all panic.

To sum up: beware of anything you didn't cook yourself and only eat it if you're convinced it came from a reputable source.

Don't forget that clean food doesn't stay clean. Raw food can contaminate cooked food and contamination can come from contact with crockery, work surfaces, cutlery or from your hands. Be sure to keep everything clean and prevent cross-contamination.

Cut, Rip, Scorch, Burn, Aaargh!!

There are lots of ways to hurt yourself in the kitchen, mostly to do with sharp edges and heat, although you could always fall off a ladder getting to a high shelf if you want. I believe in sharp knives and I think that, paradoxically, they can be safer than blunt ones. First: sharp knives are obviously dangerous so we take more care with them (but make sure they are well out of reach of children.) Second: blunt knives need much more pressure to cut with so you're more likely to slip and cut yourself. Food processor blades can also be surprisingly dangerous because they're very sharp but they don't have proper handles. Use a proper chopping board with your knife and make sure you keep your fingers out of the way.

There are countless opportunities to scald or burn yourself in the kitchen. Don't forget that cooking utensils can get hot in a microwave oven from heat conducted out of the food and if you switch from microwave only to combination cooking the utensils will definitely get hot. Microwaves can have other strange effects: for example, thick, viscous liquids like custard or porridge can erupt violently and spurt hot liquid in your face and something quite cool on the outside can have a scalding hot interior.

When you're handling hot things from the oven or on the stove you must always take a few simple precautions. Assume everything is hot all the time and only lift it by proper handles or with an oven glove; never touch bare metal. Make sure you know where you're going to put whatever you've picked up and make sure the space is clear. Use both hands for anything heavy.

3

MEASUREMENT AND THE MYTH OF PRECISION

Why Are Recipes Precise?
Perhaps the most difficult thing about doing your own cooking is that the recipes in books seem so precise. They have good reasons for this but you don't need precision for good cookery.

We've all been in the situation where we've just eaten something fantastic and have asked for the recipe only to find that the cook doesn't have one. When pressed further they might say that they 'just threw a few things together' or something like that.

If you want to pass on a recipe you have to be precise. It's no good saying 'half fill the old jug that your mother gave you' or 'add just enough' or 'put in a handful'. Recipes in books are trying to be foolproof so they give measurements as accurately as they can. They also give dire warnings such as 'Do not mix Metric and Imperial measures in one recipe, they are not compatible'. The problem is that the recipe is trying to tell you exactly what to do without room for mistakes (this is, of course, impossible).

The recipe controls the relative proportions of the ingredients and the total quantity at the same time. The relative proportions of the main ingredients are what gives the dish its structure and substance while other ingredients, in much smaller quantities, influence the taste. If this were the only thing that mattered then all recipes could be written like the ones for cocktails. In a typical cocktail recipe the measures are given in 'parts', which are of no fixed size, the only rule is that each part is equal. It's also taken for granted that the measures are volumes of liquid and not weights. It would be difficult to write all recipes with all the measurements in 'parts' because some are more easily measured by weight and some by volume. There is also a large range of quantities to be dealt with, from a 'pinch' to a 'pound', so, if a 'pinch' were a part, a 'pound' would be about a thousand parts and we'd soon get bored counting them out.

The total quantity is important for two reasons. The first is to end up with the right quantity to feed a certain number of people and the second, and more important, is so that the recipe can include instructions about cooking. As I'll explain later, the cooking time and method depend on the size and shape of what it is that you're cooking so the recipe can only tell you how to cook something if it has pinned down the size. It's often when you try to change the total quantity, for example to feed more people, that the recipe falls down. This is why Mrs Beeton's recipes aren't much good for people living on their own. Quite often the total quantity is controlled by one ingredient which can't be easily subdivided, such as an egg, so you're stuck with a certain number of eggs and the rest follows.

Inconsistency in ingredients is quite a problem for recipes. Most ingredients are complex natural products and they don't grow the same every time. Herbs and spices will vary in the strength of flavour and vegetables will vary in taste and texture. The taste and texture of meat and fish will depend on all manner of influences that happened while the creature was alive and also after it was turned into meat. Even an item as manufactured and controlled as flour will vary in its ability to absorb water and in the proportion of that all important component, gluten.

What's In A Name?
All recipes have names so that you can ask for the same thing again and know what to expect. The precision of recipes is linked to this need to label and repeat the same thing every time. The more precise or individual the name the more accurately the dish has to be reproduced. 'Curry', for example, has some meaning but leaves plenty of room for improvisation whereas 'Chicken Vindaloo' or 'Lamb Korma' leave little room for manoeuvre. If a great chef gets to name a dish not only does it have to be reproduced exactly the same every time but he might also keep some or all of it secret so it is only he (and it probably is he and not she) who can make it properly.

Named dishes are the jargon of cookery and they sometimes disguise quite simple food. Names are the way food snobs show off how clever they are without actually knowing anything.

Freestyle cookery gets you out of the tyranny of named dishes and lets you do whatever you want. Improvised food doesn't have, or need, a name but you can name the dish yourself if you want – I usually call mine 'Dinner'.

Dealing With Dumb Machines

Once you've had a bit of practice at improvisation you'll find that you get an eye for quantities and you won't need to weigh or measure precisely because you'll be able to tweak the amounts as you go. The only time when it's really essential to measure accurately is when you are working with dumb machines. Just as you can't have a vague recipe when you are telling a person what to do, if you're using a machine you have to be absolutely precise.

To illustrate this I'll give you an example. I make my own bread (I'll talk more about bread making in a later chapter) and I started out making it all by hand. However, I'm a lazy type so I bought a bread making machine. When I was doing all the work by hand I could adjust the ingredients as I went along so, if the mixture was too dry, I could add water, if too wet I could add flour. Also I'd keep an eye on the dough rising and bake it when it had risen enough. The machine isn't clever like that; it works on a fixed, timed sequence of mix, knead, raise and bake. So, if the mixture isn't right, it won't allow for it by maybe giving more or less rising time. The only way round this is to measure accurately but, even then, inconsistencies in the ingredients and differences in such things as room temperature mean that the end result can vary.

How To Measure Stuff

When you do measure things you have to decide whether to measure weight or volume and then which units to use. If you read recipes you'll find all sorts of units and you'll need to understand them if you're going to improvise on their themes. You might also find that you have equipment to measure using one set of units but you want to use another set so you'll need to do rough conversions.

I'm old enough to have grown up with both imperial units (pounds, ounces, pints, feet and inches) and metric units (grams, kilograms, litres, metres and millimetres). I find that imperial units are often easier in cooking because most of the main ingredients are in the range of one to twelve ounces, which is much more friendly than 30 to 300 grams which is the (very rough) equivalent. The other advantage of the imperial system is that it is based on division into halves so it is relatively easy to convert from proportions to weights. This is why there are 16 ounces in the pound and why most scales show ½ and ¼ ounces.

The metric system is simpler than the imperial because there's only one unit for weight and only one for volume. The unit of weight is the gram and the unit of volume is the litre. It looks complicated because there's a standard prefix for each multiplication or division by ten and these prefixes are used for all units. Here are a few of the prefixes:

milli- divide by one thousand
centi- divide by one hundred
deci-   divide by ten
deca-   multiply by ten
hecto- multiply by one hundred
kilo-   multiply by one thousand

The ones that are used in real life are kilo for kilogram, milli for millilitre and millimetre and centi for centimetre. There are lots more prefixes to go much smaller and much bigger but I won't bother you with those.

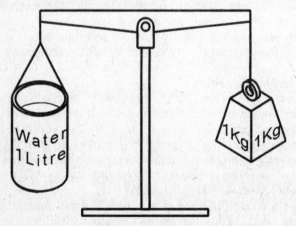

Fig. 1   1 litre of water weighs 1 kilogram

The best thing about the metric system is how easy it is to go from weight to volume because one litre of water weighs a thousand grams (one kilogram). This only works for water or anything of about the same density as water. You can tell if something is the same density as water because it only just floats. For example, cooking oil is less dense than water so it floats and one litre weighs about 800 grams. Converting this way isn't so good for pourable solids, such as flour, because the density varies but it lets you make an educated guess.

The metric system has another trick up its sleeve: one cubic centimetre (that's the volume in a cube where each side is one hundredth of a metre long) is the same as one millilitre (one thousandth of a litre) and these are often used interchangeably. So 1 cubic centimetre (cc) equals 1 millilitre (ml) and, if it's water, it weighs 1 gram (g).

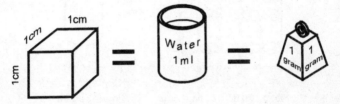

Fig. 2   1 cubic centimetre equals 1 millilitre which weighs 1 gram

You can convert from weight to volume in the imperial system but it's not so easy. The best way is to use the fluid ounce which is (near enough) the volume of one ounce of water. For some reason, lost in the mists of time, an imperial (English) pint is twenty fluid ounces while a US pint is sixteen.

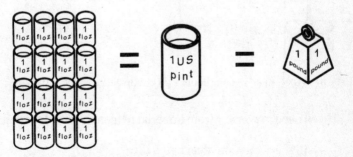

Fig. 3   16 fluid ounces equal 1 US pint which weighs 1 pound

Looked at this way the US pint seems a lot more sensible than the imperial one because it's not as easy to subdivide twenty as sixteen and a US pint is a sort of fluid pound. This is also the easiest way to convert from imperial to US volumes because the fluid ounces are (almost) the same. When you get to bigger volumes the imperial units make a bit more sense because a gallon (eight pints, equals 160 fluid ounces) weighs ten pounds. If you're using US units a handy tip to remember is that the US quart (two pints) is very close to one litre.

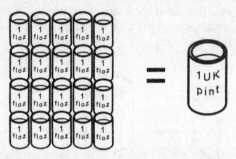

Fig. 4   20 fluid ounces equal 1 UK (imperial) pint

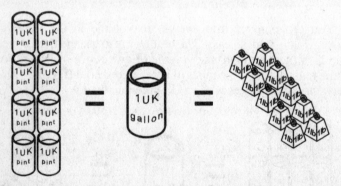

Fig. 5   8 UK (imperial) pints equal 1 UK gallon which weighs 10 pounds

If you need to convert from imperial to metric remember that:

–   a pint is a bit more than half a litre
–   a pound is a bit less than half a kilogram

- an ounce is between 25 and 30 grams
- four ounces are a bit more than a hundred grams.

Or, if you want it the other way round:

- a litre is a bit less than two pints
- a kilogram is a bit more than two pounds
- a hundred and twenty five grams (an eighth of a kilogram) is about four ounces.

There are also measures used only in cookery and you might need to convert these.

- A teaspoon is five millilitres, so a teaspoon of stuff would be about five grams.
- The tablespoon is a mess: the Australian tablespoon is twenty millilitres (exactly four teaspoons); the British tablespoon is 17.7ml (about three and a half teaspoons); the US tablespoon is 14.2ml (less than three teaspoons). Avoid tablespoons if you can.
- A US cup is eight fluid ounces (half a US pint) which is a bit less than an Australian cup which is 250 millilitres.
- A bottle, as used for wine, is 700 or 750ml (¾ of a litre)

Hotting It Up

There are two temperature scales in common use, one that makes sense and one that doesn't. They are fahrenheit (F) and centigrade or celsius (C). For those of you who don't know it, on the fahrenheit scale water freezes at 32°F and boils at 212°F, which isn't very useful for us cooks. Whereas, in centigrade, water freezes at 0°C and boils at 100°C which is much easier to work with.

When Herr Fahrenheit invented his thermometer and put a scale on it he wasn't being perverse. He chose as his zero point the lowest temperature he could reach with the technology of the time. He did this by mixing a kind of salt with ice. Salt lowers the temperature at which water freezes so the ice melts. But the melting ice takes heat away so everything gets colder until it is so cold that the salty water freezes which, in this case, happens to be 32 degrees lower than the temperature at which pure water freezes. For his 100 degree point he chose the temperature of the human body which he realised is pretty constant. Unfortunately he got it a bit wrong so the normal temperature is now accepted as 98.4°F.

The centigrade scale is just as old as the fahrenheit and was invented by a guy called Celsius which is why scientists name the scale after him, even if nobody else does. So 'C' means either centigrade or celsius depending on who you are talking to (fortunately, it doesn't matter because it's the same scale anyway). The zero of the celsius scale is defined as the freezing point of water and the 100 degree point is the boiling point of water. I think Celsius got it right and I'm going to use his scale as much as I can. The mystery is that people, especially the English and the Americans, persevered with fahrenheit for so long.

Places To Visit On The Temperature Scale		
	degrees F	degrees C
Temperature where Fahrenheit and Centigrade are the same (useful for trivia quizzes)	-40	-40
Lowest temperature Fahrenheit could reach	0	-18
Water Freezes	32	0
A nice comfortable room	70	21
Human body temperature – 'Blood Heat' (it was meant to be 100°F)	98.4	37
A nice hot cup of tea	150	66
Water Boils	212	100
Oil is hot enough for frying chips (very important!)	400	200
Red hot	900 to 1800	500 to 1000

4

WHEN IT'S BROWN IT'S DONE, WHEN IT'S BLACK IT'S BEGGARED

Heavy Philosophical Bit

Cooking is one of the things that separates humans from other animals. Wild animals are always controlled by the availability of food and their bodies and behaviour are adapted to whatever food is around. We humans are not specialised to eat particular foods but we'll have a go at anything and, because we're intelligent, we've found ways of turning some pretty unpromising materials into food.

One of our main uses of our intelligence is to find and prepare food. As individuals our intelligence enables us to choose a healthy balanced diet and to modify the raw materials we find about us into something edible. As a society we've developed culture, which is the ability to teach other people, especially our own children, to enable us to pass on what we've learnt. In fact we've become so good at feeding ourselves that in modern, developed civilisations most of our intelligence is put into enjoying ourselves because it's so easy to get food and shelter. Even cooking has become as much a leisure activity as a means of survival.

What's The Point Of Cooking?

Cooking is our most important method of changing stuff to make it edible. There are ways of preparing food that don't use heat, such as pickling, but mostly our food is cooked. Cooking does three things:

- – it makes food safer and easier to digest
- – it changes the structure and texture of food
- – it changes the taste of food

Cooking was probably invented to make normally poisonous food safe to eat. Some vegetables, such as red kidney beans, are quite deadly if eaten raw but very nutritious if cooked. I often wonder how many people died of kidney bean poisoning before they found out just how long you had to boil them (the beans, that is, not the people). By the way, you need to boil dried kidney beans vigorously for at least 15 minutes and then throw away the water to be safe and they still need to be cooked for a further hour or so to make them edible.

When civilisation started, people began to store food and it started to go off. Cooking food that is on the turn can kill the bugs and make it, relatively, safe to eat. In fact with things like game and cheese people got a taste for food which was a bit off.

Humans aren't very well equipped to eat raw food; about all we can manage is fruit, nuts and insects, although we seem to have gone off insects lately. We can eat raw meat but we don't have the teeth and jaw muscles to chew it easily so any quantity is hard work. We can't eat grass or leaves because we haven't got the complex digestive systems that animals like cows, sheep and even rabbits have.

Even if we can digest it most raw food is pretty hard work to eat. Cooking usually has the effect of softening food and making it easier to chew. Some products of nature, notably wheat, are unpromising as food but when prepared, sometimes in complex ways, and then cooked, something wonderful happens to the structure. I'll devote a chapter to wheat flour and baking later on.

The thing that we notice most about cooked food is its taste. Cooking affects taste in two ways: it causes chemical reactions in the food and it allows flavours from different ingredients to mingle. The chemical reactions are the most interesting thing and the ones we like best – the browning of meat and the frying of chips – happen at quite high temperatures.

Cold Cooking
Applying heat isn't the only way to prepare food; there are some cold techniques such as pickling, salting, smoking and drying.

These all developed out of preserving food before freezers were invented. Cooked food goes off as quickly or quicker than raw food so cooking wasn't much help for keeping food but cooking can make old, dodgy food relatively safe and palatable. Unfortunately bugs (bacteria and fungi, if you want to be posh) are happiest in the same conditions that we humans are happy, although they usually like it a bit damper than us. The trick with preserving food is to change the conditions so that the bugs that cause decomposition are killed off or, at least, don't reproduce. A few bugs won't do most of us any harm but a large number will cause the runs, or worse. Some food also deteriorates by reactions with air and light and may need to be sealed up and kept in a dark place.

Keeping the food cool stops the bugs from growing and reproducing which is why fridges are so successful. Some bugs are tough enough to continue to grow even in the cold of the fridge so the food eventually rots. Fridges are also very dry so food needs to be wrapped to stop it drying out. You might find that stuff still dries out even if it's in a plastic bag because, although the plastic can hold liquid water, water vapour can get through.

If you go further and freeze the food then it's even more difficult for the bugs to grow and it's fair to say that they don't. Bugs like to live in liquid water and they are not at all happy in ice. Some really tough bugs survive freezing, although none of them can reproduce at these temperatures. This is why there are dire warnings against refreezing food that has been thawed out. Each time the bugs get to room temperature they reproduce like mad. If you thaw the food out, cook it as soon as it's thawed and eat it while it's hot the bugs will have had very little time to reproduce so there won't be many of them. If you do that all again or if you leave the food warm at any stage then the bugs get lots of time to bonk and there may be enough to make you ill. If freezing were invented now, instead of over a hundred years ago, it's likely that it would be banned because of the health risk. There would be people saying things like 'What if the freezer breaks down?' and 'How can you tell if food has already been frozen and defrosted?' and 'How can you be sure that frozen food has been cooked through?' just like they do with any new process now. But, since we've got used to frozen food, nobody is too worried.

Freezing has an effect on the taste and texture of food apart from killing or slowing down the bugs. The main one is caused by the water in the food changing from liquid to solid. As ice forms it grows sharp edges that cut the fibres of the food and turn soft things, like strawberries, to mush. Occasionally you can make use of this if you want to soften food. The thing that's best about freezers is ice cream and sorbet (these would be very nasty if the water hadn't turned to ice). They don't turn into a solid block of ice because ice cream is stirred to stop the ice crystals sticking together and sorbet has a foam of egg white to do the same job.

Pickling uses an acid, usually vinegar, to stop the bugs growing. The food is preserved as soon as it's put into the acid but it takes a while to sink in so a pickle is usually left for some time – hours to days depending on the recipe. Although pickles were invented as a necessity, to keep food when it wasn't in season, people like the taste and texture so things are still pickled even though there are other ways of preserving them. Acid also stops the browning of fruit and vegetables that you get when they are in contact with air. You don't need a strong acid to do this: a sprinkle of lemon juice is enough.

Salting removes the water from food and bugs don't like that either. If you have a solid dissolved in a liquid, salt in water for example, and you have two solutions of different strengths next to each other then the solid bits flow from the strong solution to the weak one until the strengths are equal. This is called diffusion and it's pretty obvious. What is not so obvious is a sort of reverse effect called osmosis. In osmosis you have two solutions of different strengths (concentrations) separated by a barrier which lets the liquid through but holds back the dissolved solids. Now a funny thing happens: the liquid moves from the weak solution to the strong one to make them equal strength. The force which makes this happen is quite strong and can pull the liquid uphill which is how trees get water from their roots to the topmost leaves. Materials that can act as a barrier to solids but let liquids through are called semi-permeable membranes, which is a bit of a mouthful, but the most important thing is that nearly all animal and plant tissues act like this. If you put food into either dry salt or brine, which is just lots of salt dissolved in water, then osmosis draws water out of the food and preserves it.

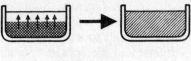

Diffusion

Dissolved Stuff goes from high
concentration to low

Semi permeable
Membrane

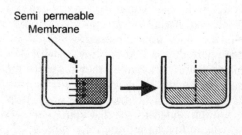

Osmosis

Liquid goes from low concentration to high

Fig. 6   Diffusion and osmosis

Sugar can work in a similar way to salt as long as the concentration of sugar is high enough. A weak sugar solution is the perfect place to grow bacteria or fungi. This is why jam has to be very sweet and why low sugar jams and preserves need to be kept in the fridge.

The oldest way of removing water from food is to dry it in the sun. This doesn't work too well in Britain but is very successful in hotter and drier climates. The dried food most familiar to us is fruit such as prunes, sultanas, currants and raisins but other foods such as meat and fish can also be dried this way. The best known dried fish is the Indian Bombay duck while South African Biltong and North American Pemmican are dried meat products. Dried food is often kept in oil which stops water and air getting at it and also changes the taste and texture because some of the oil is absorbed.

Pulses such as beans, peas and lentils dry very well and they were a major part of the northern European diet in the winter because they would keep for months. Some of them, particularly Haricot beans, dry on the stalk if they are left alone. The dried pulses can be difficult to use because they have to be soaked for a long time and then cooked for a long time. The actual soaking and cooking times depend on the bean but a rule of thumb is to soak for at least 3 hours and boil for at least 1 hour. Small hard pulses like chick peas need a lot longer, at least twice those times. I've already warned you about the dangers of red kidney beans – they need to be boiled vigorously for at least 15 minutes, for safety, before you even start the 1 hour cooking time – but you should also know that soya beans need to be boiled for at least an hour to destroy an enzyme that would otherwise interfere with your digestion. On the other hand pulses in tins are perfectly safe as they are, as well as being a lot more convenient. As far as I can tell they taste just the same as reconstituted dried beans.

Smoking is another way of removing the water from food by drying but it has the added effect that some chemicals in the smoke are poisonous to the bugs so the food is doubly preserved. As usual, you can't get something for nothing, as it seems that some of the chemicals are poisonous to people too and can cause cancer but the occasional kipper or bit of bacon shouldn't do you any harm. Depending on how it's done, smoking can be hot enough to cook the food or just enough to dry it a bit. Curing is a bit like smoking but the chemicals are injected or soaked into the food. And, as if to make it more complicated, food is often cured and then smoked. Both smoking and curing are done mostly for taste nowadays rather than for preservation and smoked and cured food is kept in cool compartments in shops and should be kept in the fridge at home because it doesn't keep all that well.

The other main way of preserving food is to sterilise it – in other words, kill off all the bugs, and then seal it up in a bug proof container. The usual bug proof containers are metal cans but bottles, cartons and bags are also used. Ordinary plastic bags won't work because gasses can get through. To stop this the plastic is coated with metal. That metallic finish on flexible food packaging isn't just for decoration, it serves a purpose. The sterilisation is usually by heat and the temperature and time needed to kill the bugs are nearly as much as are needed to cook the food. That's why sterilised and UHT milk taste different from ordinary milk and why canned foods taste different from fresh.

Another way of sterilising food is to use radiation. This is the same radiation as atom bombs and nuclear reactors so it worries a lot of people. There's enough radiation to kill the bugs but not enough to make the food radioactive so there's no risk to health from that. The technical rather than emotional concerns about irradiating food are similar to any other preserving technique being mostly that some food is changed in flavour or texture. (Apparently a very few foods taste quite nasty after irradiation.) Another concern is that it's difficult or impossible to tell if food has been irradiated. This worries some people as it may make it possible to pass off old food as fresh. Personally, I think not being able to tell if food has been irradiated is a good thing, but you can't stop people worrying by using logic.

Once the sealed package of sterilised food is opened the bugs can get in and the food begins to deteriorate just as if it were fresh so it needs to be eaten quickly and kept in the fridge. The sealed pack also keeps out air which can cause some spoilage by reacting with the food.

Freezing, salting, pickling and jam making are things you can do at home but canning is a bit impractical. The home alternative is bottling in which you use an airtight glass jar to store the sterilised food.

Why Is Cooking So Difficult?
To really understand cooking we'll have to do some physics and I'll try to make it as painless as possible. The aim of cooking is to raise the temperature of the food. To raise the temperature of anything you pump heat into it. Heat comes from burning things like gas, wood or coal or from electricity.

Electricity isn't really anything material in itself, it's just a way of moving energy about. You turn electricity into heat by forcing it to go through a material that it doesn't go through easily. The heating rings in your cooker are like that and the electricity has such a struggle getting through that it makes the rings hot. Because it resists the flow of electricity this kind of material is called a resistor.

Materials that don't resist much are called conductors and materials that resist a lot are called insulators. The water in food is an electrical resistor so it's possible to cook some foods by passing electricity through them. The technique is called

'Ohmic Heating' and it's used in industrial food preparation but it's pretty impractical for home use. To use electricity for cooking at home you need to turn it into heat or microwaves.

Once you've got your heat you have to get it to the food and this is where all the different cooking methods like grilling (broiling in America), baking, roasting, boiling, steaming and frying come from. Heat travels in three different ways:

- it can move through a material (like electricity does)
- it can travel through space (like light does)
- it can be carried in something which is moving (like a hitchhiker does)

Just like electricity, heat travels more easily through some materials than through others (in fact it's often the same materials: for example, metals transmit both heat and electricity while plastics do not). The other similarity with electricity is that this way of moving heat is also called conduction. If you try to pass heat through a material it doesn't want to go through (an insulator) it's slowed down and takes longer to get through than it would in a material it travels through easily (a conductor). This is important for cookery because most foods are insulators so it takes a long time for heat to travel into the middle of the food.

Heat can also travel as radiation. The word radiation has had a bad press lately from its association with atom bombs, nuclear power and nuclear waste. Most radiation is harmless and essential, the bit we sense directly is light but we are also familiar with radio, infra red, ultra violet and X rays. These are all the same thing but at different frequencies in the 'Electro-Magnetic Spectrum'. If you had a magic radio that could tune in to the whole of the electro-magnetic spectrum you could tune from ordinary broadcast radio through shortwave and television broadcasts and out into microwaves (I'll come back to them later) through infra red and into light from red to blue. In that direction you continue into ultra violet to X rays and gamma rays. The important thing about all this is that heat can travel as infra red radiation and that infra red is a lot like visible light.

Heat can travel by being carried in a hot gas, usually air, or a hot liquid which for cooking is water or oil. When heat is moved about this way it's called convection. I'll explain how convection works when I tell you about ovens.

Striking The Balance

To cook something we have to get it to a certain temperature and keep it there for a certain time. The actual temperature depends on what effect we want; something delicate, like a meringue, needs a low temperature but, if we want the chemical reactions that make interesting flavours, then the temperature must be high. The difficult bit is getting the middle of the food hot enough without getting the outside so hot that it burns.

Heat will only flow from something at a high temperature to something else at a lower temperature. If you sit a hot cup of tea on top of an ice cube the ice cube will warm up and melt and the tea will cool down. You'll never find the tea getting hotter and the ice getting colder.

Most cooking uses a source of heat which is at a much higher temperature than we want the food to be. In fact, you don't get much infra red radiation given off until something is at least red hot, like an electric heating ring for example. If the food were to reach the same temperature as the heat source it would be burnt to a frazzle. The trick with cooking is to take advantage of the inefficiency of the heat transfer to expose the food to the heat for the right length of time for it to reach the temperature we want.

The Open Fire

The simplest way to cook is to hold the food up in front of a fire. It's easy to imagine stone age hunters doing just that with their catches and then drooling over the cooked meat. The grill and the barbecue are just slight modifications of this to make it more convenient for us modern folk.

Anyone who has used a barbecue, and to some extent a grill, will know how difficult it is to balance the heating of the outside of the food with the inside. This is because grilling uses infra red radiation to heat the food and the radiation doesn't penetrate into the food. So while the infra red rays merrily heat up the surface very quickly it takes a relatively long time for the heat to conduct its way into the middle of the food.

Fortunately, cooking the outside more than the inside is just right for many foods such as beef. The outside gets to a high enough temperature for all the taste making chemical reactions while the inside stays as near raw as we like. If you want the food to cook evenly then you have to slow down the heat input to the surface to give time for the heat to conduct into the food.

Alternatively, you can make sure that the distance from the surface to the middle is short; in other words you cut stuff up thinly. Another trick is to use something which does conduct heat, such as metal, to heat the middle of the food. This is the purpose of the skewer in kebabs.

The difficulty with a barbecue is that it isn't really very hot. The cooking is done after the flames have gone out and the only heat is that retained in the charcoal, which is much less than red hot, so it takes quite a long time to cook anything. If you look at a grill you'll see that it's red hot either from the direct heating of the electrical element or from the flames playing on a metal or ceramic grid in a gas grill. If you take your cooking times from your experience with a grill it's no surprise that everything from the barbie is underdone.

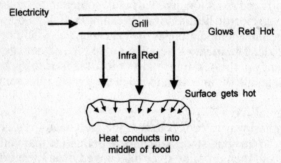

Fig. 7 How a grill works

Being a gadget freak I use an electric barbecue which puts out the same heat as a grill but allows the meat juices and fat to drop onto hot stones to give the special tastes and smells that we expect from cooking over an open fire.

The Closed Fire
In the early days of western civilisation, when the first stone and brick buildings were being made, people started bringing fires indoors and putting them in boxes. These were the first ovens and they were very important because they were available just when bread became the staple diet. It's very difficult to cook bread on an open fire but easy in an oven.

Once the fire is enclosed, the heat is carried mainly by hot air and radiation is less important. Air is a pretty useless conductor of heat but it can move the heat about by actually moving itself. This is called convection and it gets a bit complicated. In a typical oven air is heated either by contact with the gas flame or by the electrical heating element near the bottom of the oven. Stuff gets bigger when it's heated but doesn't get any heavier so the hot air floats to the top of the cooler air. This moves the heat from the flame or element to the top of the oven which is why the top is the hottest place even though the heat is put in at the bottom.

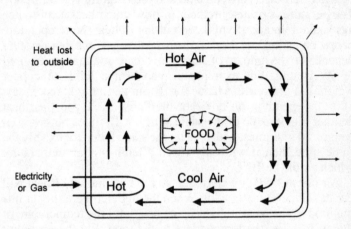

Fig. 8   How an oven works

The air at the top cools down as it gives up its heat to the food and to the walls of the oven so it gets pushed down by more hot air coming up from the bottom. Ovens are fairly airtight so the same air keeps going round and round getting hotter and hotter and heating the food more and more. The temperature is limited by a balance between the heat going out through the walls of the oven and the heat being put in by the fuel or electricity. This means that you can control the temperature by turning the heat input on and off which is exactly what the thermostat does.

When you pre heat an oven you heat up the oven walls and the air inside. This gets the temperature balanced out and means that the food starts cooking as soon as it's put in the oven. You want this because some foods, such as meat or cakes, need their surfaces heated quickly to seal them and slow down the loss of moisture. The high temperature on the surface causes chemical changes in the food that make it more waterproof and stop water from escaping too fast.

The advantages of the oven are that it can cook over a very large range of temperatures, it's easy to control the temperature, you can walk off and leave it without anything terrible happening, and it doesn't use much fuel if it's well insulated. The problem with the oven is that it's slow because, although air can reach high temperatures, it can't carry much heat.

The difference between heat and temperature is a bit tricky. Temperature is a measurement of how much heat a substance has soaked up and if you keep putting in heat the temperature keeps on going up. For a given heat input, the temperature depends on the amount of stuff that's there and that's measured by its weight. For example, if you heat a lump of copper weighing 1 gram with a flame for 10 minutes it might reach, say, 100°C, depending on how hot the flame is. If you then heat another block made of the same stuff but 10 times bigger, so it weighs 10 grammes, with exactly the same flame for exactly the same time then it will only reach a tenth of the temperature which would be 10°C.

Air doesn't weigh very much so a small amount of heat will put its temperature up a lot. When the high temperature air hits the food in the oven it gives up its heat until the temperature of the air matches the temperature of the food. But the air didn't have much heat so it doesn't have much effect on the temperature of the food. To get the temperature of the food up you have to move a lot of air. Each little bit of air carries a little bit of heat and eventually the food heats up.

In a normal oven the speed at which the air will move is fixed. It only depends on the time that it takes for the hot air at the top to cool down and sink. When the air stops moving the only heat transfer is radiation from the walls of the oven which is pretty low because the walls aren't very hot (not red hot anyway) and by conduction through the air. Conduction through air is a non starter compared with convection; remember that trapped, still air is the insulation in most of our clothes and it works very well.

The technical fix to this problem is the 'Convection Oven'. This really ought to be called the 'Forced Convection Oven'

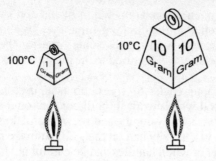

In the same flame for the same length of time
the lighter block gets to a higher temperature

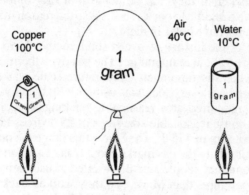

But the same weight of different
stuff gets to different temperatures

Fig. 9   Heat versus temperature

because all ovens use convection. In these new fangled inventions a fan forces the air to move round much faster than it would by natural convection so it can move heat more quickly. This speeds up the cooking and has the side effect of evening out the temperature in the oven so there isn't much difference between the top and the bottom. This can be a disadvantage because when you get to know a normal oven you can cook different things at different temperatures at the same time by placing them at different heights.

Pre heating isn't so important with convection ovens because the air is pushed around so fast that it doesn't have much time to lose heat to the oven walls. Convection ovens don't make all that much difference to the cooking time, they're about 10 to 20% quicker, because it still takes some time for the heat to transfer from the surface of the food to the inside just like it does with the grill.

There are various tricks to speed up heat transfer to the middle of the food which work in both conventional and convection ovens. I've already mentioned skewers and these can be used in the oven just as they can on the grill but make sure they don't have plastic or wood handles and be careful not to pick up the food by the skewers with your bare hands (but then you're not that stupid, are you?). Cakes can be made thin so they cook through quicker or they can be made in a ring mould which doesn't have a middle to cook. This is also the reason that bagels and doughnuts have holes in them.

Because of the history of ovens some recipes have a funny way of talking about temperature. The gas oven thermostat was invented when the fahrenheit temperature scale was the bees knees (that means everybody was using it). So the guys designing the thing started at a reasonable cooking temperature of 275°F and chose reasonable size steps of 25 degrees fahrenheit up to a maximum of 475°F. They gave this range the numbers 1 to 9 which is where the gas marks come from. Later on the oven makers found that people actually wanted to use their ovens at lower temperatures than Mark 1 so they worked backwards in fractions which isn't very scientific but it's what they did. This is all a bit more clear if you look at the table opposite.

In this modern technical age we like to see something more scientific-looking in our kitchen so the manufacturers started putting actual temperature values on the oven controls. This is fine with fahrenheit as there's an exact relationship between the gas mark and some fairly friendly numbers. With centigrade it's a mess. I've shown, in the table, the exact conversion from fahrenheit to centigrade for each gas mark but that isn't what you see on the dial of an oven with centigrade numbers. To make it look nice the numbers are rounded to the nearest 10 but every now and then there needs to be a jump of 20 to catch up. All of this is pretty pointless anyway as the thermostats are notoriously inaccurate and yours could easily be as much as a whole gas mark out.

Just in case all this is too technical the oven temperature is sometimes described in words, as I've shown in the last column of the table, but I don't think any oven has these words on the dial so you'd have to translate into numbers anyway.

The Wonderful World Of Oven Temperatures					
Gas Mark	degrees F	degrees C exact conversion	degrees C as shown on ovens	Temperature step in degrees C	Description in words
¼	225	107	110		Very Cool
½	250	121	120	10	
1	275	135	140	20	Cool
2	300	149	150	10	
3	325	163	160	10	Moderate
4	350	177	180	20	
5	375	191	190	10	Moderately Hot
6	400	204	200	10	
7	425	218	220	20	Hot
8	450	232	230	10	
9	475	246	240	10	Very Hot

Getting Into Hot Water
Next to air, the most convenient stuff for transferring heat is water and it happens that water is very good at it.

When you raise the temperature of something you put heat into it but some substances need more heat than others to reach the same temperature even if it's the same weight of stuff. So, even if you had the same weight of copper, water and air and you heated them with the same flame for the same time they would all reach different temperatures. Of course it's hard to visualise this because the volumes would be so different but believe me it's true. To predict the temperature you need to know how much heat you're putting in, the weight of stuff that you're going to heat up and another number that depends on what it is you're heating. The fudge factor that techies, like me, use for these serious thermodynamic calculations is called the specific heat capacity and it's different for different materials. The specific heat capacity is the amount of heat you have to put in to raise a *specific* weight of material a certain temperature. Copper has a low specific heat capacity while that of water is about ten times higher; air is about halfway between the two.

But all that doesn't matter right now, the important thing is that water has a high specific heat so it can carry a lot of heat for its weight. The downside of this is that if you want to raise the temperature of water you have to put in a lot of heat which is why a watched kettle never boils (well it does boil really but it takes a long time).

So, when you put food into hot water, the food soon reaches the temperature of the water because the heat transfer is so good. This doesn't make any difference to the heat transfer inside the food from the surface to the middle which is why a good insulator, like a sponge pudding, still takes a long time to heat through.

The thing about water is that it stops being water if it gets too hot because it turns into steam. This means that you can't get the temperature of the water above its boiling point. If you keep putting in heat you won't raise the temperature any more, instead all the heat gets used up turning the water into steam (that heat is called 'latent heat', by the way).

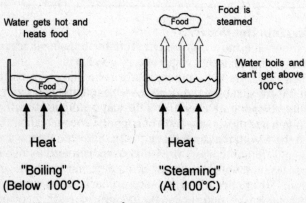

Fig. 10   Cooking in water

The temperature of boiling water is nowhere near high enough to cause the chemical reactions that give those lovely crunchy brown tastes but it's high enough to have some effect on taste and texture. At these temperatures the fibres in meat soften and red meat turns brown (this brown is similar to the brown you get at high temperatures but it's not the same). Fish changes from its slippery raw texture to a drier flaky one. In some vegetables, such as potatoes, the stuff they are made of, called starch, blows up and turns fluffy.

Another thing about water is that it makes things wet. A lot of foods absorb water which is a technical way of saying that they get soggy. Quite often that's just what's wanted for preparing foods that have been dried like pasta, rice or beans. Drying food is a good way to preserve it and we are so used to it that we sometimes forget that drying isn't natural. Heat helps the food absorb water and this, like most things, can be overdone which is why vegetables get revoltingly soggy if they are cooked for a long time.

Natural foods are complex mixtures of chemicals, some of which dissolve in water. This can be a good thing if they are poisonous or bad tasting but bad if they are nice tasting and nutritious. The trick is to cook for long enough to get rid of the bad stuff but keep the good stuff. Usually you throw away the water with all the dissolved stuff in it but sometimes the whole point is to get the flavour and nutrition from the food into the water as when you make soups and stews. Some vitamins (especially vitamin C) dissolve in water and boiling vegetables also destroys the vitamins in them. Personally I wouldn't boil vegetables because steaming or microwaving does a much better job.

Most boiling isn't really boiling at all as it isn't necessary to have the water that hot. That's just as well because it would take a lot of heat to keep water on the boil and it would fill the kitchen with steam. Normally the water is kept just below boiling; you can see the surface of the water moving but there are no steam bubbles breaking the surface. This is called simmering and it's fairly easy to control with a gas cooker but difficult with electric. With gas you can balance the actual heat input by controlling the size of the flame but it's different with an electric ring. An electric ring is controlled by a device that automatically turns it on and off. When you set the knob it just controls the proportion of the time that the ring is on. When the ring is off the water gets too cold and goes 'off the boil'. So you turn it up. Next the ring promptly comes on at full power and the pot boileth over. It's even worse with the lid on because you can't see what's happening and there's less heat loss so it boils over quicker.

Even Hotter Water

Cooking at 100°C is pretty slow so there are ways of bumping up the temperature a bit.

You can cook in steam instead of water (it's called steaming – clever huh?). Steaming needs special equipment to hold the food out of the water and in the steam. There are some nice electric and plastic gadgets on the market to do just that or you could improvise. Steaming is excellent for vegetables, partly because there isn't so much water about to soggify them.

Steam carries heat in a special way. When it lands on something cold it turns back into water and gives up the heat that it needed to turn from water to steam in the first place. This is that latent heat again and it's a much more efficient way to carry heat than ordinary convection.

You can put your food above a small amount of water in a closed container in the oven to get it to steam and this is called shallow poaching or pot roasting. This method is good for cheap cuts of meat and was probably invented because the early ovens were part of the house heating, so they were on, at least at a low level, all day. Nowadays other methods such as an electric slow cooker or a microwave might be more appropriate and cheaper in fuel.

The steam isn't much hotter than the water it came from. To get water and steam to higher temperatures we need to increase the pressure. Increasing the pressure increases the temperature at which water boils. This is reasonable because all the surrounding air makes it harder for the bits of water (molecules, to us techies) to escape and become steam. As you apply heat to the water the first bits of steam get out. As you put in more heat more steam comes out and, if you close the lid on your pot tight enough, it builds up pressure in the pot making it mc ⸱ difficult for the rest to boil. This would go on for ever, as long as you keep feeding it heat, except that the pot would go bang, so real pressure cookers have valves to let the pressure out when it's high enough. This is the function of the weight that you put on the top of the pressure cooker and when it's bouncing about it's doing its job of controlling the pressure.

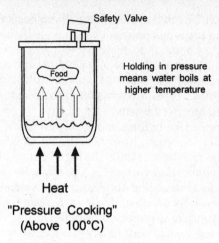

Safety Valve

Holding in pressure
means water boils at
higher temperature

Food

Heat

"Pressure Cooking"
(Above 100°C)

Fig. 11   Cooking at pressure

Usually you only put a small amount of water in the pressure cooker, just enough to make all the steam you want, and you are really cooking the food in superheated steam which is quicker than in boiling water (superheated means that it's hotter than boiling water at normal pressure). If you put in too much water it takes a long time to get to the boil and wastes a lot of the time that you would have saved by using the pressure cooker. Pressure cookers are a bit quicker than simple boiling but if you include the time to get up to pressure and the time to cool down enough to open the lid safely they aren't much of a time saver.

Really Hot Stuff
The thing we humans really like is brown food. There's something special about the taste of food that has been heated enough to go brown. It's caused by a bunch of chemical reactions which are different for different foods but it's a pretty reliable guide that brown is good. Unfortunately, brown isn't very far from black and black doesn't taste very nice at all. Cooking in water can't get anything brown like this because the temperature can't get high enough. What we need is a liquid that will get hot enough without boiling away or bursting into flames and that isn't poisonous.

This is where oil comes in. Cooking oil can be raised to nearly 200°C without too much problem which is easily hot enough to brown food. Any hotter than this and it will decompose and taste nasty, and if it gets really hot it will burn and you'll get an exciting chip pan fire. By the way, the only difference between oil and fat is that fat is solid at room temperature and oil is liquid, otherwise they are just the same.

Deep frying is like boiling, using oil instead of water, and, just like boiling, the main heat transmission is by convection. Because of the high temperature, the high volume of oil and the speed of the convection currents it's possible to move a lot of heat into the food in a short time so frying is quick as well as tasty. Deep frying is a violent affair so delicate foods, like fish for example, need some protection which is the main function of batter or breadcrumbs. Fortunately the fried batter or breadcrumbs taste good too.

The main thing that slows down the cooking is our old friend water. If there's any water in the food it has to boil away before the food can get higher than 100°C and this takes up some of the valuable cooking time. If all the water were boiled away the food would be dry and horrible. Fortunately, frying is so hot that it can cause chemical reactions in the food that turn the surface waterproof (this is called sealing) so the surface is dried out and the inside can stay moist.

As usual the timing is critical. You have to get the surface hot enough for long enough for the interesting reactions to happen before the inside gets too hot and dries out. Deep frying works best if it's quick so it only works on pieces of food which are not very thick. If you want to deep fry something relatively thick like a doughnut, for example, you need to use some tricks. This is why doughnuts either have holes in them so that there isn't an uncooked middle or they are filled with jam which doesn't need to be cooked. Chicken Kiev works in the same way as a jam doughnut with the butter in the chicken replacing the jam.

Just as some foods absorb water, some absorb the oil and this can be good or bad. Usually a small amount of oil absorbed into the surface tastes nice and improves the texture but a large amount absorbed deep into the food is a bit slimy and definitely bad for the health. The way to make sure that the least amount of oil is absorbed is to get the oil hot, dry the surface of the food and use fresh oil.

Out Of The Fire Into The Frying Pan

Another way to get heat into food is to sit it on top of something hot. The something is usually the metal base of a saucepan or frying pan. The metal is heated by radiation from the gas flame or the electric ring and, because metal is a good conductor, the heat travels very quickly from the underside of the base of the pan to the top surface. The tricky bit is getting the heat from the metal of the pan into the food.

If the food is liquid and moves about fairly easily then it will spread itself over the pan and get hot. However, the metal is at a high temperature and has heat pumped into it at high speed so the surface of the food in contact with it cooks so fast that it easily burns. Burnt food not only doesn't taste good but it's also very sticky and it doesn't conduct heat very well. This means that any part of the food that starts to burn sticks to the metal surface so it won't move. After this it gets even hotter and more burnt because it can't conduct heat away. All this is bad so it's essential to stir the food to stop any part of it starting to burn. You only have to do this with liquids that don't flow easily (cooks call these liquids thick and scientists call them viscous) because thin liquids, like water or oil, will stir themselves, by convection.

If the food is dry it will only cook where it touches the metal and it will quickly burn in those places and get hardly any heat into the bulk of the food. The usual way to deal with this is to shallow fry on a thin layer of oil. The oil fills in the gaps where the dry food isn't touching the frying pan and heats the food by conduction because there isn't enough liquid for convection to get going. This gives a much bigger surface to conduct through so the heat transfer is much better.

The food can still stick because oil isn't a very good conductor of heat and some parts of the food are still touching the hot metal surface and will get burnt. You've got to move the food around to stop it sticking and you can do this by pushing it around with a spatula, or something similar, or you can shake the pan and make the food jump about. That's why the French call this method of cooking 'sauté' which means 'to jump'. The oil also gets between the food and the metal of the pan and helps to stop the food from sticking to the metal. It does this because a liquid can't stick two solids together unless it sets into another solid.

The other way to stop the food sticking is to coat

the metal with a special solid surface that the burning food can't get a grip on. This surface is a plastic called Poly Tetra Fluoro Ethylene (PTFE to its friends). Teflon is the trade name for the same stuff. The gimmick with PTFE is that it forms a smooth surface, it doesn't melt at cooking temperatures and it doesn't like reacting chemically with anything. This last bit is important because the stickiness of food is mainly a chemical reaction with the surface of the pan. The bad thing about PTFE is that it's soft so it can easily be scratched off the surface of the pan. We are so keen to make cleaning easier that we put up with this and use tools and scourers that are made of plastics which are as soft as the PTFE and won't scratch it or wear it away. More recent non stick surfaces still use PTFE but the metal underneath is bumpy so that the tops of the bumps protect the PTFE coating from scratching.

With all the concern these days about healthy eating and keeping your weight down frying is rather out of favour because the food always absorbs some oil which makes it much more fattening. If you use a non stick pan you can quite often get away with not using any oil at all. Just because the food isn't sticking doesn't mean it's cooking evenly so you still have to keep it moving about. Alternatively you can often grill or bake instead of frying.

Cooking With Radar
Cooking with microwaves is different from other kinds of cooking because of the way the microwaves interact with the food. Technically a microwave oven is most like a grill because microwaves are a kind of radiation, like infra red heat but at a different frequency (remember the magic radio tuner?). The big difference is that, while infra red rays are stopped at the surface of the food, microwaves penetrate some distance inside. Food is, to some extent, transparent to microwaves but opaque to infra red. If food were completely transparent to microwaves you wouldn't be able to cook with them because the waves would go right through and out the other side. Fortunately for the micro-wave oven manufacturers it happens that there's a good balance between the amount of energy that gets through food and the amount that stops in the food and makes it hot.

Microwave ovens use the technology that was invented to make lightweight radar for aircraft during the Second World

War. In fact, the early American ovens were called 'Radar Ranges' which is a name I like a lot. I also like to think that the use of radar for cooking was discovered because birds passing through the beam of high power radar and radio transmitters were found dead on the ground and appeared to have been cooked in flight. But I might be making that up.

Microwave ovens are much less wasteful of energy than ordinary grills because the metal walls of the microwave oven reflect the waves almost perfectly and the waves bounce around inside until they hit the food. In a grill the infra red waves spread out in all directions and heat up everything they meet, including the grill pan, the rest of the cooker, the kitchen and you. The only thing in the kitchen that reflects infra red well is very shiny metal. The fact that metal reflects microwaves almost perfectly has a few side effects. The best known is that you can't use metal cooking containers because the waves are reflected off the container and never reach the food. Worse than that, if you're unlucky, the reflected waves can damage the part of the oven that generates the microwaves (which goes under the grand name of 'Cavity Magnetron').

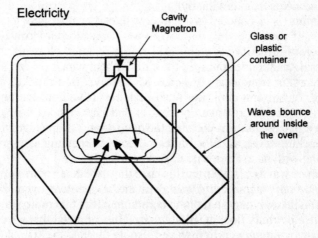

Fig. 12   How a microwave oven works

The microwaves bounce about so perfectly that they can completely miss some areas in the inside of the oven which means that any food in those areas won't get cooked. This is why most microwave ovens have a turntable to move the food around or, in the few that haven't got a turntable, there's some device to scatter the microwave beam. Even with the turntable or the beam scatterer there can still be cold spots which is why you should turn the food over or stir it at least once during cooking. This doesn't happen with a grill because, instead of being reflected, the infra red waves are absorbed by the body of the grill and re-radiated as more infra red. Since the infra red is coming from all directions it's very unlikely that you'll get any cold spots.

Another fortunate thing is that many materials such as glass, ceramics and many plastics, are completely transparent to microwaves. These materials make excellent cooking pots because all the energy gets into the food instead of heating up the pot. The oven manufacturers have a bit of a problem with this because they know we like to look inside the oven to watch the food cook. However, a glass window would let the rays out which would be wasteful and would cook people's eyeballs. To get round this the glass window is covered by a metal grid which has holes big enough to see through but small enough to stop the microwaves from getting out.

Safety is a concern with microwaves because people are made of the same stuff as food so we also absorb microwaves and get hot inside. We are used to the dangers of traditional cooking techniques because they all use heat which we can feel on our skin from a safe distance. Microwaves don't make your skin hot but can cook the flesh underneath without warning. This is why microwave cooking is done in a closed box and nothing happens until you shut the oven door. The leakage from a working oven is tiny, unless there's something seriously wrong with it, so there's no risk to your health.

Microwaves also remind us that they are like radio waves when you put pieces of metal in the microwave oven. The reason that we can use radio to communicate is that radio waves make electricity flow in suitably sized bits of metal that we call aerials or antennae. Microwaves also do this and the size of the aerial is about 25 – 250mm (one – ten inches). If there are any bits of metal in the oven they will act as aerials and electricity will flow in them. If the bits are part of a closed loop, electricity will flow round the loop and make it very hot. If there are any small gaps in the loop the electricity will jump across as big, juicy sparks. None of this is any good for the bits of metal or for the microwave oven. Now, most people don't put bits of metal in their microwave oven deliberately but sometimes we make mistakes. The usual one is to forget the gold decoration on the best dinner plates. This will go bang and spoil the plate. The other mistake is when there's some metal in packaging that we didn't know about. I once didn't notice a sort of metal staple closing a bag of food. It took quite a while to find out where the sparks were coming from and I finally worked it out when the staple got very hot and melted the bag.

The fact that the microwaves penetrate into the food has a big effect on cooking. The first and best known effect is that it's much quicker. As I explained with the grill and the conventional oven the outside surface of the food is heated first and it takes some time for the heat to penetrate into the bulk of the food. With microwaves the heat is put straight into the middle of the food so you don't have to wait for it to penetrate from the surface. The depth that the microwaves get into the food isn't fixed, the energy just drops off with distance until there isn't much effect. As a rule of thumb assume that the microwaves get about 10 – 20mm (½ – 1 inch) in, after that the heat is back to travelling by conduction.

It's often said that microwaves can't brown food. This isn't exactly true, although it might as well be. What actually happens is that the microwaves cook the food so evenly that the outside surface doesn't get much hotter than the inside. If you allowed the food to cook for long enough the outside would get hot enough to brown but the inside would be dry, tough and totally inedible. I know, I've done it! In fact the food gets so dry that if it's left in for a little longer it catches light and burns.

I'll tell you a story about overcooking food in a microwave oven. I used to work in an office where we had the use of a microwave oven to cook lunch. The office was on two floors and there was only one oven which was downstairs. A secretary, whom I shall call 'S', was cooking a potato for her lunch. S was based upstairs so she went downstairs and put her potato in the oven and set the oven for 10 minutes. After a while S phoned a bloke, whom I shall call 'B', whose desk was near the oven, and asked him to check her spud. B said it wasn't cooked so S asked him to put it on for a bit longer. B said 'How long does it need?'

and S said 'About 10 minutes' meaning the complete cooking time from the start should be 10 minutes. B, not knowing this, put the spud back in for another 10 minutes on top of the time it had already had. The spud dried out and burst into flames. This set off the smoke detectors which set off the building fire alarm which automatically called the fire brigade who turned out with two engines and lots of hunky firemen.

Meanwhile we all had to evacuate the building and stand around outside until the firemen said it was OK to go back in. This was lunchtime and S had an exam to go to so she left without any lunch before the fire engines got there. The next day S told me that she saw the fire engines passing her bus on her way out. The lady sitting next to her had said 'There must be a big fire somewhere' and S replied proudly 'Yes, I know, I started it!!'

The unusual feature of a microwave oven is that it has a timer. I know conventional ovens have timers but timing isn't very critical with them whereas it is with a microwave oven. Most cooks aren't really interested in exact cooking times, they just cook until it's done. Because browning isn't practical in a microwave oven it's hard to know when the food is cooked and the cooking times are a lot different from what you may have been used to with a conventional oven. The way to get the timing right is to read the book that comes with your microwave. You should also read what it says about cooking times on food packaging, experiment for yourself and, if you're really organised, make notes.

Although a microwave oven is called an oven and, as I've explained, it works more like a grill, I find it best to think of it as if it were a pressure cooker. It doesn't work anything like a pressure cooker but the way it cooks is very similar. The fact that the pressure cooker cooks by hot steam means that it puts a lot of heat into the food without it being in contact with lots of water or oil and at a temperature above boiling water but below that of hot oil. The microwave generates heat inside the food and especially heats the water that's in there so it sort of makes steam inside the food. The heat transfer is also very good. The big plus with a microwave, compared to a pressure cooker, is that you don't have to wait for the steam pressure to build up before the cooking starts and you don't have to wait for the pressure to drop to safe levels before you can open the lid.

Everybody knows that you use a microwave oven for defrosting frozen food. Well, that's true, but it's not all that easy. If you try to defrost food using ordinary cooking techniques you'll definitely cook the outside of the food before the inside even gets warm because the food is a good insulator of heat. This is demonstrated in the gimmick dessert called 'Baked Alaska' in which ice cream is wrapped in meringue. Because the meringue is an exceptionally good insulator and cooks at low temperature it's possible to cook it before the ice cream melts. You get just the same effect when you defrost something except this time it isn't what you want.

Microwaves are much better than conventional cooking for defrosting but there are still problems. Most books tell you that the microwaves vibrate the molecules of liquid water and make it hot but have less effect on the solid ice. This is probably true but I think latent heat is pretty important too. Just as when you heat water you have to put in extra heat to turn it from water into steam so when you heat ice you have to put in extra heat to turn it into water. The microwaves penetrate into the frozen food and heat up the water at the same time as the ice but, while the ice is absorbing heat to change from solid to liquid, the food is getting hot and starting to cook. The way to deal with this is to keep turning the microwave power on and off. The food heats up while the microwave is on and the heat flows by conduction from the hot bits of food to the cold ice while the microwave is off. When microwave ovens were first available you had to stand there with your finger on the switch turning it on and off but you don't have to nowadays because it happens automatically when you select low power or defrost. If the food is thicker than the microwaves can penetrate (that's about 50mm (two inches) because the microwaves can get in from both sides) then defrosting is much slower because all the heat transfer into the middle is by conduction.

After all this you probably just want me to tell you what you can cook in a microwave oven and what you can't. Well, in my experience, it's fantastic for the kind of puddings that you have to boil for ages. You can cook a Christmas pudding or a haggis about twenty times faster in a microwave than by putting it in boiling water. It's excellent for melting fatty things like butter or chocolate. It's magic for vegetables, as I explained earlier in the bit about boiling. It's perfect for fish but very fast so you can easily overcook.

When microwave ovens were new the favourite trick was to cook jacket potatoes in them while going on about how quick it was. This probably put more people off microwave ovens than anything else because the result tastes nothing like a jacket potato from a conventional oven. What you get is a potato boiled in its skin, which is OK, but not what you expect from an oven. Another trick is to cook sponge cakes which whoosh up to be incredibly fluffy in seconds. Unfortunately, they are dry and don't taste too good.

Microwaves are useless for cooking meat because meat needs to be browned or it tastes very boring. There are things called browning plates which are based on the assumption that once you've got a microwave oven you don't use anything else to cook with. If you live in a bedsit without a grill, hob, frying pan or oven they might be worth using, otherwise they're a waste of time.

The browning plate is technically quite interesting as it's the opposite of what you usually want from a microwave cooking container. Instead of letting the microwaves through to heat the food the browning plate is made of stuff that absorbs the microwaves and gets very hot itself. This means that it acts as a frying pan or hot plate inside the microwave oven. It does work but it's messy and quite difficult to use. An alternative, which was quite common in the early days of microwaves, was to coat the meat with some stuff that either started off brown or turned brown during cooking. This is a waste of time, don't bother. If you want to cook meat with microwaves get a combination oven.

The Radar Ranger Meets The Conventional Kid
Since everyone had done the baked potato trick and had tried to cook their Sunday roast in their microwave oven, and had been deeply disappointed on both occasions, the boffins had to invent a cooker which would actually do all that had been promised. This was the combination oven which can use heat and microwaves at the same time. The combination microwave oven has a fan assisted convection oven or a grill, or both, built into it. For cooking meat and dishes such as pies and pizzas the combination oven is excellent. The main limitation is size as most combination ovens are too small to put in a large joint or turkey or anything like that.

To recap what I told you before: the infra red radiation of the grill or the hot air of the oven only heat the surface of the food and the heat travels into the middle relatively slowly; the microwave radiation penetrates into the food and cooks it fairly evenly all the way through. There's no reason why these two things shouldn't happen at once and that is exactly what happens in the combination microwave oven. The outside surface of the food gets a double dose of cooking from heat and microwave while the inside gets cooked by microwave without having to wait for the heat to travel through from the surface. This means that roasting really is quicker but there's still a balancing act to do. For one thing, you can't take advantage of the inefficient heat transfer to cook the surface of a steak, for example, while leaving the middle nearly raw (which is how I like it), because the middle will be cooked by the microwaves.

The fact that cooking is significantly faster can fool you into leaving it too long because 'it can't possibly be cooked already' but, on the other hand, a large joint will still take a while to cook because the microwaves don't penetrate much more than an inch into the meat. Fortunately, because the food is being browned during cooking, it's fairly safe to say that 'if it looks done it is done'.

Combination ovens are a bit tricky to use because you have so many choices: you have to set the microwave power level, the temperature and the time and, if you want to make it really complicated, you can change the settings during cooking. The best way to get a feel for what to do is to use the instructions and cooking settings supplied with your oven. After a while you'll be able to make intelligent guesses as to what the setting should be. Until you're sure, keep an eye on the cooking; you can always turn it off before the timer is finished. If it's not done you can put it back for a bit longer.

Usually when you're using heat with microwave you set the microwave to half power or less otherwise the inside will cook so quickly that the outside won't have time to brown. I usually find that, with the combination oven set at maximum temperature and medium microwave setting, the cooking time is about a half to two thirds what you'd expect in a conventional oven and you don't have to pre heat.

For pies and pizzas and other similar dishes, where you want to cook the filling at the same time as the pastry or bread base, the combination oven scores again. With a normal oven it can be impossible to cook this kind of dish in one go, you usually have to cook the base separately before you add the filling and then cook the filled pie for a bit longer. With a combination oven you can set it so that the microwaves cook the filling while the heat cooks the pastry or bread. I often cook an apple pie in this way in fifteen minutes using variations on the recipe that came with my combination oven.

I've tried baking bread and cakes using combination cooking, mostly because I'm very impatient with conventional ovens, but I've found that although they cook all right, and very quickly, they tend to be dry and taste stale.

Combination microwave ovens are more complicated and more expensive than ordinary microwave ovens but I think they're worth it. If you are buying a combination microwave oven you should watch out for a few things. First make sure that what you're looking at really is a combination oven. Some microwave ovens that just have grills are being described as combination ovens. These are OK but they are not as versatile as a combination oven which includes a fan assisted conventional oven, although they are cheaper. Secondly, don't get more gimmicks than you need. This is true of ordinary microwave ovens as well but it's worse with combination ones. The sort of things you might see are press button controls, digital displays, automatic cooking settings, temperature probes and weight controlled cooking. All of these are supposed to make things easier but, quite often, they are harder to use than simple controls because you have to trick the machine into doing what you really want. If you're not sure that you want a feature then you probably don't need it so save your money and buy a cheaper, more basic, model.

Someone I know bought a top of the range combination microwave oven for his wife believing, reasonably enough, that the most expensive is the best and that the best is what she would want. This oven is so complex to operate that the instructions are in a book about twenty pages thick and are supported by a video. You can't just press a couple of buttons and set it going, you have to program it with your requirements first. This has put his wife completely off using this very fancy piece of kit and off the whole idea of ever trying a new piece of kitchen machinery again.

My Way

From all this you can probably tell that I'm a believer in microwave cooking; in fact, I use two. I have a combination microwave oven which I use for meat, pies, pizzas, jacket potatoes and that sort of thing and an ordinary microwave oven that I use for vegetables, fish, casseroles, canned food and stuff. To prepare a meal I often start something cooking in the combination oven and use the ordinary microwave to heat up vegetables to go with it. My favourite trick is to use the delay timer on the ordinary microwave to start its cooking at the right time so that both ovens finish together.

The two microwaves are so successful that I don't use a conventional cooker at all. Instead I have some gadgets for special jobs like a deep fryer, an egg boiler, an electric steamer, an electric barbecue and an electric kettle. It's worth remembering that the usual kitchen cooker consists of several cooking devices in one unit, typically four heating rings, two ovens and a grill. So it's no wonder that you need more than one microwave to compete with that lot. If you're building a kitchen from scratch and don't already have a cooker it's worth considering the microwave route because a set up like mine costs less and takes up less room than a conventional cooker.

I have some other gadgets that I actually use instead of leaving in the cupboard (although I've got plenty of those too). I've already introduced you to my bread machine which I use regularly because I can make the kind of bread you can't get in the shops. I also have a pressure cooker that goes in the microwave. I use this to cook brown rice because it needs boiling for a long time and this technique cuts it down to about twenty minutes. I use an electric egg boiler because it does perfect eggs, either soft or hard, and you don't end up with a scaly saucepan. I use one of those cheap, plastic, electric steamers for vegetables 'cos it cooks them perfectly.

I found the grill of an ordinary cooker quite difficult to replace and I've ended up with a few gadgets to do its job. I've already told you about my electric barbecue which is great in the summer when I can use it outdoors but it's really far too smoky to use inside. I used to live in an upstairs maisonette and although I had a garden it was a long walk to get to it so I tried using the barbecue in the kitchen. It was just about bearable if I opened all the windows and had the extractor fan on full power but it's not the sort of thing I want to do often.

My all-singing, all-dancing, combination microwave oven has a grill as well as a convection oven and I do use that sometimes but it's not as powerful as a conventional grill. Most recently I treated myself to a new gadget called a vertical grill. This is simply a large toaster redesigned to cook meat and other similar things. Instead of a pop up mechanism there's a removable, hinged, metal grid which encloses the meat or whatever and stops it sliding down to the bottom of the toaster. The insides are removable for cleaning and there's a drip tray to catch the fat and juices. This thing works very well. It's quicker than a normal grill because it cooks from both sides at once and it's more energy efficient because the insides are shiny metal and reflect the infra red waves.

And, last but not least, I've an electric kettle for those endless cups of tea.

Is It Ready Yet?

If you're fairly new to this cooking lark you probably haven't much idea of how long you should cook things. Even if you've been cooking all your life you might not know how long things take in terms of minutes and seconds because you just keep cooking until it's cooked and you instinctively know when that is. Surprisingly enough the cooking time doesn't depend all that much on what you're cooking, it mostly depends on the cooking temperature, which in turn depends on the cooking method, and on the size and shape of what you're cooking.

You choose the cooking method to suit the stuff you're meaning to cook. We've already talked about how heat travels through the food by conduction and that some foods conduct heat faster than others. The aim is to get the middle of the food hot enough for long enough to cook it. This means that the cooking time is related to the time it takes for heat to travel to the middle of the food. The heat moves quicker if there's a big difference between the temperature at the surface of the food and the inside. We haven't much to play with here because if the surface temperature is too high the food will burn. If the food is thin or in small pieces the heat doesn't have far to travel so it gets to the middle in a short time; if the food is large like a cake or a joint of meat the time is much longer.

We can start to see a pattern now: if something needs to be

cooked at a low temperature then it needs a long time while at a high temperature it cooks much quicker. Boiling and steaming are at the low temperature end so you usually need to cook things for at least half an hour. An exception to this are foods that only need heating up rather than cooking. The cooking of raw ingredients such as meat and vegetables takes ten to twenty minutes once the food is heated through but stuff like pasta doesn't need any more than heating through so five to ten minutes is enough.

Anything you can cook on a grill has to be thin so it only takes about ten minutes to cook once the grill is up to its full temperature. Don't forget to turn the food over so it cooks both sides. The first side will take longer than half the time and the second side less because it's already started to heat through. You can reckon on about seven minutes for the first side and three for the second but all this is only for interest because you always keep an eye on what you're grilling and stop when it gets brown. If the food starts to burn before the time you expect then turn the heat down and let it cook slower.

Shallow frying is pretty much like grilling as far as timing is concerned but deep frying is a bit different. Deep frying is very hot and hardly anything needs more than a few minutes but dense foods like meat or potatoes may need longer (for example, chips take about fifteen minutes). Cooking in an oven usually takes a long time, even if the temperature is high the heat transfer is slow because of the low heat capacity of the air. Just about anything you cook in an oven takes at least an hour, although something very thin such as a sandwich cake could take less than half that. Likewise anything really big, like a turkey, may need many hours at a lower temperature.

As I've already explained, microwaves are different from heat waves because they can dump energy directly into the food without having to heat up the surface first which means that thin foods cook very much quicker and two or three minutes is often enough. The trouble is that this can be misleading because if the food is a bit thicker the microwaves don't get all the way through to the middle and you have to wait for heat conduction just like with ordinary cooking. Once the food is thicker than a couple of inches the cooking times are more like conventional cooking and a large piece will take twenty to forty minutes.

All this assumes that the food is at room temperature. If it's

frozen the cooking doesn't start until the ice has all melted and
this can take a long time. The safest thing is to thaw out food
thoroughly before you start to cook it. If you're organised
enough to get the food out early enough then you can let it
defrost by leaving it standing at room temperature for a while.
An ordinary lump of something will take an hour or two but
something big like a turkey may take up to twelve hours. Don't
forget to keep the food covered up while it's defrosting to stop
the bugs getting at it.

If you defrost with a microwave you've still got a problem
with heat transfer but it's much quicker than leaving food to
stand at room temperature. You need to use a low or defrost
setting and you need to turn the food over at least once during
the process. Something small and thin can usually be defrosted
by about six to eight minutes in a microwave while something
bigger may need as much as twenty minutes to half an hour.

So, how do you know if the food is cooked? We've already
talked about browning, which is pretty important, and burning,
which tells you you've gone too far. You can detect both of
these by smell as well as sight so trust your nose. Some food
such as cakes or large joints of meat can be brown or even black
on the outside but raw in the middle. The trick with these is to
stick a skewer in. In a cake the skewer will come out dry if the
cake is cooked. With meat look for the colour of the liquid that
comes out: if it's red then the meat isn't cooked. With beef
we've got a problem because it tastes best if it isn't thoroughly
cooked but still a bit red in the middle. If you're worried about
food poisoning but want rare beef then you'll probably have to
be scientific and use a roasting thermometer. You'll need to
make sure that the middle of the joint has reached at least 70°C
for a few minutes. All the books say that no other meat should be
eaten uncooked and who am I to contradict them? I sometimes
feel the skewer with my fingers to see if it's hot, especially with
frozen food that might not have thawed in the middle, the
skewer will also tell you if the middle is still frozen solid.

Remember, if any red liquid comes out when you stick the
skewer in, the meat isn't cooked and you run a risk of food
poisoning, especially with poultry. In fact, if any meat, apart
from beef, is still red in the middle it needs to be cooked for
longer and even with beef you're taking a chance.

With other foods the change in texture shows that they are

cooked. One famous trick is to knock the bottom of a loaf of bread: if it's cooked it sounds hollow. With spaghetti the thing to do is to pull out a strand and try it between your teeth: if it's still hard or very chewy it's not ready, if it's soft and squidgy you've overdone it and if it's just a bit chewy it's just right. The Italians call it 'al dente' when it's right and 'dente' means teeth. You can do the same sort of thing with vegetables: if the texture's right, they're cooked. You can check this with a fork or try with your teeth but be careful or you'll be scalded on the delicate mouth parts. I find that jacket potatoes are ready if the skin has lifted from the flesh of the potato and is hard and crackly – you can feel this with your fingers if you're quick (if you hold on too long you'll get burnt).

Things like stews and sauces often have a very obvious change. What you need to look for here is that everything has gone a similar colour and consistency. If the ingredients still all look separate then it probably isn't ready. Minced meat seems to disappear into the background when it's cooked. Most of the time if it looks right it is right.

5

HORSES FOR COURSES

10 Million Recipes

There must be millions of recipes in the world but I can think of
only four ways to prepare a dish for cooking. These are:

1. Cooking a single ingredient
2. Cooking a mixture of ingredients
3. Putting one lot of ingredients inside or on top of another lot
4. Baking

Of course, when you make a meal it's more complicated than
this because you'll probably need to use a few of these methods
at once. There are so many different recipes because there are so
many variations on each theme. Each of the methods can be
used on different main ingredients and can then be modified by
different flavouring ingredients so, if you multiply up all the
options, you can get into the millions quite easily. The following
sections cover the methods I've listed above, except for baking
which is so complicated it gets a whole chapter to itself.

How To Cook An Egg

Some ingredients can be cooked on their own without any
messing about. This includes most meat and fish, most vegetables and eggs.

Meat can be grilled, barbecued, fried or roasted but usually
the smaller and more tender cuts are used for grilling, barbecuing and frying while the larger joints are roasted. This is simple
physics. As I explained in the bit about cooking methods, a large
piece of food needs to be cooked for a long time at a relatively
low temperature to allow time for the heat to get to the middle

but a small piece can be cooked fast and hot. The tougher bits of meat, which are usually the cheapest, are best cooked slow and wet in plain water or in a stew or casserole or as a pot roast.

Compared to meat, fish needs very little cooking although it does need to be cooked through or it tastes slimy and any bugs that might be in there won't be killed off. An oven is too hot and too dry for fish, although it's possible to bake fish if it's protected in a roasting bag or wrapped in aluminium foil or paper (this is called 'en papillote', in yer actual French). Grilling and barbecuing are OK but can be difficult because the fish easily falls to pieces. It's best suited to steaks cut from big fish like salmon or swordfish or to big flatfish like plaice or flounder. Frying, either shallow or deep, is good but the fish usually needs to be protected against drying out by coating with breadcrumbs or batter which also helps to stop it falling apart. Steaming or poaching (which is pretty much the same thing) is good, particularly for large fish and, as usual, the microwave is excellent but you have to be careful because the fish will cook in seconds.

Eggs are unusual in that although they start off liquid they set very easily, with a small amount of heat, to a jelly-like solid. This means that you can get away with some cooking techniques that you couldn't use if the eggs stayed liquid. Don't be fooled, it isn't easy to cook an egg and I wouldn't recommend it as an exercise for beginners. Obviously you can boil an egg in its shell but you can also cook it by dropping it straight into boiling water, which is what some people mean by poaching. If you do this the outer layers of the egg white set almost immediately and hold the insides in place while the cooking continues. You can use soup instead of water to poach the egg: traditionally the Chinese drop the egg into the soup while the Italians pour the soup over the egg. When you fry an egg the heat of the pan sets the white quite quickly which is why it doesn't flow over the whole frying pan. The yolk has a membrane around it that holds it in shape and makes that dome in the middle of the fried egg.

Some books about using microwave ovens go on about ways of cooking eggs in a microwave. If you try to cook eggs in their shells by microwave they will explode, so don't do it. You can boil eggs in a microwave oven by wrapping them in aluminium foil and covering them in water. The foil stops the microwaves from getting at the eggs but heats the water which heats the eggs as if they were in a saucepan. This is obviously a stupid way of cooking so only do it if you've no choice. You can make a kind of scrambled egg if you just put a beaten egg into a suitable container and zap it with the microwaves on full power for a short time, less than a minute. The eggs will blow up to three or four times their original volume so make sure the container is big enough. I've found that it's best not to add anything (such as butter or seasoning) as it seems to stop the eggs from rising.

Vegetables are traditionally boiled but many can be baked or included in stews and casseroles. Potatoes can be cooked in just about any way you can think of: baked in their skins as jacket potatoes, roasted in the oven, deep fried as chips, shallow fried as sauté, boiled, pressure cooked or microwaved. I don't think potatoes are usually grilled but I bet somebody's tried it. (You can also bake other vegetables in their skins, I've tried onions and beetroot and they were pretty good.) In Japanese Tempura any kind of vegetable is deep fried in batter, often at the table, but it seems that only tough root vegetables like potatoes are strong enough to be deep fried without batter (that's chips or 'pommes frites' in case you haven't worked it out yet). I've also had some success with deep fried parsnips (we call parsnips snarpips at home, because we're silly, so deep fried parsnips are 'snarchips'). And, finally, don't forget: you can't beat a steamer or a microwave for cooking vegetables.

The thing to learn from this is that you can cook just about anything any way you want, there isn't a 'right' way to do anything. The only limitations are practical ones: you can't grill an egg because it would dribble through the grill rack before it set. To be perverse, someone has usually worked out a way to cook anything using any method which is why some of the procedures are a bit complicated. Somebody said 'A man with a hammer thinks everything is a nail'. It's the same with cooking. If you've only got an oven you cook everything in an oven. Sometimes these complicated techniques, like en papillote, for example, give a different taste or texture so you might use them even if you don't have to.

The other thing to learn is that plain cooking can be very good. You don't have to do anything complicated to make a good meal – the classic meat and two veg can be excellent if it's done right. Before you get involved in fancy recipes try cooking your ingredients as simply as you can. This way you'll learn what food really tastes like and you'll have a basis from which to start making things more complicated if you want to.

Irish Stew (In The Name Of The Law)

The next most complicated thing after cooking whole single ingredients is to cook mixtures. You might do this for various reasons: to combine flavours, to change the texture, for convenience or to cut down on the washing up. Usually mixtures have at least one liquid or semi liquid component. If all the ingredients were dry there wouldn't be much point in mixing them because they'd stay separate anyway, although there are some dry mixtures, such as Bombay mix, used as snacks.

Mixtures can be very wet, as in soups and stews, or almost dry as in meat loaf or burgers. If the mixture has enough solid content it's possible to make layers which I think is mostly done for appearance, it doesn't seem to do much for the taste.

Soup can be made from just about anything by boiling it for long enough. Obviously, some things work better than others but, if you're in an adventurous mood, you could try anything. Soup is traditionally made from leftovers and offcuts and is usually based on a mysterious thing called 'stock'. Back in the olden days nobody wasted anything so all the inedible food like bones, fish heads and bits of vegetables were thrown in a pot and boiled for hours or days until they sogged down into a liquid which had all the taste of the stuff that had been thrown in. Every now and then they would strain off the liquid and use it to make soups and sauces. Today it seems odd to do this because fuel and time are more costly than stock cubes but a hundred years ago there would have been a range or stove heating every house so it was natural to keep a stock pot simmering all day. There would also have been someone in the kitchen to watch the pot and stir it occasionally. Stock cubes are OK but, compared to the real thing, they're very salty and a bit artificial.

If you're making a stock specially, rather than just being thrifty, then you should keep some control over the stuff you throw in. There are fish stocks, poultry stocks and meat stocks and they don't really mix. I'm not an expert on this so I won't give any advice other than to say have a look in some recipe books for ideas or experiment and see what happens.

The stock straight out of the pot was too watery for most purposes so another trick was born: the liquid was boiled for a while which drives off the water leaving the tasty stuff behind. Since the volume is made less this is called 'reducing' the stock. You can use this technique whenever you want to concentrate flavours and make food less watery. Water is usually the stuff that boils off first (technically that means it's the most volatile) but if there's any alcohol in there it will boil off before the water. You can use this to control the booziness of a dish. Concentrated stock has a very strong flavour and is the basis of a lot of French style cooking.

To make a soup you can either boil stuff up as if you were making stock or take some concentrated stock and add liquid to it, it all depends on what you are trying to achieve. The tastes and textures are different but they're both soup.

Soups can be thickened in two different ways, one is by using flour (which I'll go into in the chapter on baking) and the other is by using vegetables or cereals. Some vegetables and cereals, like lentils, peas, potatoes, rice and barley, turn to mush if they're boiled long enough. Usually that's a really bad thing but in a soup it gives a thick, rich texture. You can thicken anything by adding cream (which I think is a cheat because it's so easy and it's seriously fattening, being almost entirely fat). You have to be a bit careful because cream easily separates and curdles but it adds instant richness to anything.

There isn't much difference between a soup and a stew, the main thing is that a stew has more lumps of food in it and you eat it for the solid rather than the liquid contents. A stew was the thing that really got me into cooking. I was on a health kick at the time and I wanted to reduce the amount of fat I was eating so I experimented with cooking vegetables. I filled a large pot with likely looking vegetables that I saw in the supermarket such as, cabbage, onion, swede, turnip, parsnip, leek, potato or carrot. At first I tried simple combinations such as carrot and onion but it soon got more complicated with cans of beans such as red kidney, borlotti or canellini, and canned tomatoes. I also tried herbs such as, oregano, basil, rosemary and parsley as well as other flavourings like garlic or chilli (I'll go into getting the flavour you want in another chapter). For a long time the concoction was strictly vegetarian, not for any convictions or principles but just as an exercise to see if I could do it. When I discovered spicy sausages, especially pepperoni, the strictly vegetarian went out the window. The point about all this is that this vegetable stew, or casserole as I called it, never had a recipe but always came out edible and was sometimes downright brilliant. I would just chuck in a load of stuff, boil it for a while and eat it. 'Nuff sed (sorry – enough said).

The sort of thing you have to watch with stews is that everything is cooked evenly, even though the different ingredients need different times. There are two things you can do: one is to cut the bits of slow cooking stuff into smaller pieces so that the heat can conduct into the middle in less time, and the other is to cook them longer. Any ingredient that needs much more cooking time should be given a special cook-up on its own before the other ingredients go in. I find that carrots and potatoes need a long time so I zap them for a few minutes in the microwave on their own or cook them in a steamer.

Put in enough water to cover everything (I did try beer or cider but it didn't seem much different so I stopped bothering) and keep the lid on. The lid recycles the steam which cools back to water on the relatively cool surface and drips back into the pot. This stops the stew drying out too fast. On the other hand, if you want to thicken the stew, heat it for a while with the lid off to drive off some of the water as steam. You can use flour, rice or lentils to thicken stews just as you can with soups. I also find that potato, cooked long enough to turn to mush, gives a nice thick consistency to stews (as you'll find in Irish stew).

A stew doesn't have a structure. In other words, it doesn't matter where the lumps are. This is very useful because it means you can stir a stew to get it to heat through evenly. Other similar dishes, like Moussaka or Lancashire hot pot, are layered so if you stir them you mess up the layering. This means you have to cook them slowly at a relatively low temperature which means you have to use an oven. For those of you who don't know, Moussaka is a classic Greek dish consisting of layers of sliced aubergine (fried in olive oil) alternated with a sauce made with mutton mince. Lancashire hot pot is similar but uses raw potato instead of fried aubergine.

A stew can be very thick but it's not usually strong enough to cut into slices unless you've made some big mistakes. If you want that kind of structural integrity you need something to bind the ingredients together and that something has to turn solid at some stage in the proceedings. Meat happens to include such a binder and it's called gelatine. The stuff that holds muscle together in living animals is a protein called collagen (I'll explain about proteins in the chapter about nutrition). Meat is dead muscle and when you cook meat the collagen turns into gelatine, provided there's enough water around. The gelatine and water mixture sets as the temperature goes down. We're all familiar with gelatine, it's what makes jelly gel. It's possible to extract the gelatine and use it to set the water in any mixture so you can have fruit jelly, meat jelly, or vegetable jelly. If the gelatine is purified then the jelly can be clear like in Chicken in Aspic. As gelatine is made from animals it's not acceptable to vegetarians. Fortunately, nature has come up with an alternative in the form of some stuff called 'Agar-Agar' which is extracted from seaweed and can be used instead of gelatine.

Fat can also act as a binder because it turns from a liquid at high temperature to a solid at lower ones. This is used in pâtés which have a high proportion of fat and in sausages which are meant to be eaten cold such as salami. Cheese has a similar effect both in the fat hardening at room temperature and in the proteins turning solid as they cool. The proteins in eggs also coagulate and set into a solid. The setting of proteins is called denaturation and it's a lot like the making of plastics. The action of heat affects the large protein molecules so that they change shape and some of them chemically link with others. The change in shape makes the molecules tangle together and the chemical cross-links stop them from untangling. Since the molecules can't move, the result is a solid. Denaturation is a permanent change and the solid won't melt if you reheat it. The various proteins in eggs, milk and cheese, when combined together and heated, will set into a firm, opaque jelly which is the basis of flans, quiches and cheesecakes.

In hamburgers and meat loaf the protein in the meat denatures and sticks all the chopped up meat back together again. Adding an egg will put in extra protein just to make sure. Hamburgers are really quite difficult to deal with because they aren't held together by anything until the protein denatures so they can easily fall apart especially on a grill or barbecue. The modern solution to this is to freeze them. The frozen water holds the burger in one piece until it's cooked enough to hold itself together and, if you're lucky, the balance will be just right and the burger will cook through without falling apart or burning on the outside. In fact it's worth freezing home made burgers even if you don't need to do it for preservation reasons.

At least burgers do stay together when they've been cooked. If you want something of the same sort of consistency without meat it's very difficult. Vegeburgers and bean burgers are usually held together by egg and maybe cheese, and mashed beans can form a stiff paste which will just about hold up under a grill. Some of the beans, especially soya, have a large amount of protein and can be formed into a kind of mince that acts a bit like meat as far as cooking is concerned. This soya protein is often called TVP (for textured vegetable protein). TVP hardly has any taste and no fat but it absorbs flavour from the liquids it's cooked in and sometimes tastes strange because of that. Treating it like meat doesn't work – it needs lots of strong flavours added and something to keep the texture light and moist.

Another product which has been sold as a vegetarian meat substitute is Quorn. This is protein extracted from a kind of fungus. (The manufacturers keep a low profile about this but we are happy to eat mushrooms which are also a fungus, so what the heck, I say!) Quorn is similar to TVP in that it doesn't have any taste of its own and it will pick up flavours from the liquids it's cooked or soaked in, sometimes giving strange results. Don't treat these products as meat but rather as a useful source of bulk and protein in vegetarian cooking. They don't help with the flavour of the dish and can in fact make it more difficult to get a good result than if you just used natural, growing out of the ground type, vegetables.

Get Stuffed

In the *Monty Python's Flying Circus* television comedy series there was a sketch about 'The Royal Society for Putting Things on Top of Other Things'. The whole point of the sketch was to ridicule the very idea that anyone would be interested in putting things on top of other things and the sketch ends with the chairman of the society admitting that the whole thing was a waste of time. He should have been a chef. In cooking we seem to be obsessed with putting one lot of ingredients on top of another lot and that obsession pales into insignificance compared with the desire to put things inside other things. Maybe it's a macho thing but any food that can have its inside scooped out will be stuffed with something else. Anything that can be stuffed will be stuffed – vegetables, meat, fruit, bread – in fact, anything that can be turned into a container will be filled with something by somebody.

Usually the stuffing has to be of a thick consistency because most of the containers aren't all that leak tight and thin stuff would run out. Any of the stuff described in the previous section, as long as it's thicker than soup, could be stuffed into something. Vegetables are usually stuffed with meat and meat stuffed with vegetables, while fruit is usually stuffed with more fruit or with some sweet dairy concoction. Containers don't have to be ready made, they can be specially made for the purpose and the most common material for this is pastry (I'll waffle on about pastry in exhaustive detail in the next chapter). Pastry is used for pies, flans, pasties and turnovers which are all the same thing apart from their shape.

I'm using the concept of stuffing loosely here. Stuffing implies some force and you don't need much force to pour a wet filling into a pie. Bread can be used in pretty much the same way as pastry but it's not as watertight.

There are several reasons for putting things inside other things. The main one is the convenience of the finished item. A pie, for example, can be carried about, easily stored, sliced and eaten in the hand but you can't do that with a stew. Another reason for stuffing is to mix flavours and textures that would otherwise have to remain separate. This happens when the pastry of a pie or the meat of a stuffed joint absorbs some of the flavour of the filling.

Some vegetables are just asking for it. A large marrow tastes of hardly anything but it's easily scooped out to make an inviting cavity just waiting to be filled with meat or vegetables. Cooked in the oven the moisture in the marrow stops the filling from drying out and the filling gives the marrow some flavour that it wouldn't otherwise have. Peppers and aubergines are similar in that they have nice inviting middles that are full of inedible seeds that are usually scooped out and thrown away. Fruit can be treated in the same way and it has become a bit of a cliche to serve orange sorbet in an orange and lemon sorbet in a lemon. Baked apples are a sort of apple pie without the pie. Not many people eat apple cores and once they are removed there's that hole waiting to be stuffed. All it needs is some dried fruit and maybe some honey or syrup, cook that for a while in the oven and you've got yourself an easy dessert.

To most people stuffing is what you put in chickens and turkeys before you cook them. Stuffing animals is an ancient tradition that was probably originally done to keep the cooked carcase in a lifelike shape when it was brought to the table for show. When the innards are extracted from an animal it leaves a cavity that is just crying out to be filled with something. Unfortunately, at least with fowl, the best place to put flavourings is under the skin; a big ball of stuff in the middle of the bird doesn't help the flavour or texture of either the meat or of the stuffing. This kind of stuffing is usually made of the same ingredients as a dumpling or sausage with a lot of herbs to give it flavour. The flavour of the stuffing should dissipate into the meat so it's made with a much stronger flavour than it would have if it was eaten on its own. Relatively boring bits of meat are often spiced up by rolling them up with some stuffing in the middle and tying the joint up with string.

Stuffing can help with the cooking process. I explained, way back in the bit about cooking methods, that it can be difficult to ensure that the inside of a piece of meat is cooked through without burning the outside. One way to deal with this is to replace the middle of the meat with something that doesn't need to be cooked so much. The stuffing is usually pretty much precooked so it doesn't need the prolonged heating that meat needs. You still have to be careful because the bugs that cause food poisoning can be carried from the meat into the stuffing and still need to be killed off by heat. Butter is an effective stuffing because it moisturises the inside of the meat and with a bit of garlic and a few herbs it tastes great. This is the basis of Chicken Kiev which also illustrates the problem of holding the stuffing in place. Chicken Kiev is made from chicken breast formed into a pocket and filled with flavoured butter, the whole lot is coated in breadcrumbs and fried. It's difficult to seal the chicken breast which means that the butter can sometimes leak, once it's melted, and all the lovely juice gets out.

A less obvious reason for putting things inside other things is the element of surprise. Some of these surprises can be on a grand scale. The nursery rhyme that goes 'Four and twenty blackbirds baked in a pie' refers to such a surprise. Apparently the blackbirds were alive and 'when the pie was opened the birds began to sing'. This was just the sort of gimmick dish the aristocracy would have expected at the time. The tradition continues to this day with the nubile young lady inside a huge birthday cake (you can't use live animals any more because people might think it's cruel). On a smaller scale there are surprise dishes like Baked Alaska, which I've already described, and the old tradition of putting a small coin (preferably a silver one) in a celebratory pudding. This latter goes back to the Persian tradition of putting surprises in dumplings.

The Pies Have It

Pies probably originated from a lack of crockery. Although you need a dish to support the pie while it's cooking you can remove the cooked pie and use the dish again. The pie becomes its own serving dish. It will stand unsupported and can be brought to the table. It saves on washing up if you eat the serving dish! A good pie will be firm and dry on the outside and soft and moist on the inside which happens to be a consistency we like very much. Organoleptic research (I like that word so much I'll say it again 'Organoleptic', it means the response of the senses) has found that the favourite combination of textures is a relatively hard exterior, that breaks under the teeth, and a soft yielding interior. As well as in pies you'll find this in confectionery bars, sweet pastries and choc ices. It may be that we like that combination because it's what you expect of a ripe piece of fruit.

Making a pie is quite a complex operation. You have to make the pastry, roll it to the right size and shape, make the filling, put the pastry base in a dish, put the filling in the pastry, put a pastry lid on the pastry base, seal the lid and, finally, cook the pie. This is a far cry from 'chuck everything in a bowl and heat it up' which is how you prepare most things.

All these stages have their problems: the pastry has to be the right consistency – not too dry or it breaks and not too wet or it's sticky and difficult to roll; the pastry has to be rolled to the right thickness – too thin and it breaks, too thick and the pie will be too stodgy and you might not have enough left for the lid; the filling has to be of the right consistency – too thin and it will leak, too thick and the pie will be dry; the cooking time has to be enough to cook the filling without burning the pastry. When I started baking pies I always had trouble with the rolling and I found the biggest help was to use a large rolling pin (the kind with straight sides and no handles) which I found much easier to control than the classic type.

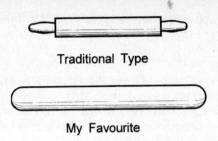

Traditional Type

My Favourite

Fig. 13 Rolling pins

Cooking pies is tricky. It would be a fluke if the pastry and the filling cooked at the same rate so you can't rely on that happening. You've got two choices: either you cook the pastry more than the filling or you cook the filling more than the pastry. If the filling needs only a short cooking time, for example a fruit pie, then you need to cook the pastry blind, that is, empty. The problem with blind baking is to stop the bottom of the pastry base from rising which it will do because of the steam trapped underneath. First thing is to make some holes in the bottom by prodding it with a knife or a fork, in fact it's worth doing this on all pies. Next put something in the pie to hold the bottom down. The traditional filling for blind baking was dry beans but nowadays you can get special ceramic beads for the purpose. If the filling would take longer to cook than the pastry, you'll have to cook the filling a bit first. The aim is to combine the filling and the pastry so that they can finish cooking together so you don't fully cook either before they are combined.

Pies are baked in an oven on a low heat so that there's time for the heat to conduct through to the middle of the filling. As I explained in the bit about cooking methods, you can cook pies in a combination microwave oven which gives you the flexibility to control how much of the heat is from hot air at the surface of the pie and how much is from microwaves which penetrate into the filling. Using this technique you don't need to blind bake.

I think that the best bit about pies is the way that the inside surface of the pie absorbs some of the juice from the filling and gets a gelatinous texture which I like. However, it's not to everyone's taste and there are some tricks to prevent it. Blind baking will make the pie crust more waterproof, especially if it's

coated with egg white before cooking, and a drier filling will
obviously help in keeping the pastry dry.

It's A Set Up

Some pies don't have lids and they're usually called flans or
tarts. Savoury flans usually have short pastry bases and the
filling includes egg and cheese so that it sets. This is also called a
quiche and we all know real men don't eat quiche but they do eat
egg and bacon flan! Sweet flans usually have a soft cake base,
while an open pie with a short crust base is usually called a tart.
If a pie has a lid it's no problem if the filling's a bit wet, it won't
go anywhere, but if there isn't a lid the filling needs to be set
solid. With fruit tarts the usual thing is to glaze the fruit with a
very thick, clear sauce made with cornflour or arrowroot or to
set the fruit in jelly. Cheese cakes are a variation on this theme
where the filling is a sweetened soft cheese mixture. Some
cheese cakes have a broken biscuit base (the bits of biscuit are
held together by butter which sets hard in the fridge) and some
have a cake base. As you can see the names aren't very important and are used indiscriminately – the same dish can be called
a pie, a cake, a flan or a tart.

Some pies don't have bases, only lids, and they have to be
served from the dish they were cooked in. This style is most
common for meat pies which are just stews with pastry lids on
(suet pastry is best). On the other hand, if the pastry making
process is stopped at the stage where it has the consistency of
breadcrumbs, and these are scattered over the top of a fruit
filling, then you've got a crumble. Tradition is strong in these
things: proper pastry goes on meat pies, crumble goes on fruit
pies. If you want to be a real rebel you could try it the other way
round. On the other, other hand, if you make the pastry into little
balls and cook them in a stew, you've got stew and dumplings.
Suet pastry and suet dumplings are exactly the same thing. They
only differ in the way they're cooked. Learning this was one of
my great defining moments – it was then that I realised that
there's more similarity than difference in the various methods of
preparing food.

Another variation of the pie doesn't have a lid or a base but
the pastry is made into an envelope to hold the filling. This is
usually called a turnover when it's got fruit in it and a pasty
when it's filled with meat. The French developed a special

pastry that blows up to make a stuffable cavity when it's cooked, it's called choux pastry and it's used for those naughty cream cakes and desserts like eclairs and profiteroles. The inside of the pastry is filled with cream or custard, or anything sweet of that consistency, and the outside is smothered in chocolate sauce. The savoury version is the vol-au-vent which is made from a biscuit size piece of puff pastry. The pastry rises but the middle is uncooked so it's scooped out and thrown away leaving space to put something in.

These Frenchified ideas seem to be convenient packages but it's an illusion, they're just made that way for show. Eclairs squirt cream everywhere as soon as you bite into them, profiteroles have to be chased around the plate because you can't cut them with a spoon and vol-au-vents have a habit of ejecting their scalding hot contents straight into your mouth just when you're trying to impress someone with your sophistication.

Other things are used to wrap food in a similar way to pastry. Pancakes are used as a wrapping for both sweet and savoury fillings. The French call them crêpes, the Russians call them blinis and I don't know what the Chinese call them but when they're deep fried we call them pancake rolls. Leaves are sometimes used to wrap stuff while it's being cooked. In Mediterranean countries it's usually vine leaves and in Africa it's banana. Sometimes the leaves are eaten, sometimes they're thrown away. In our modern, civilised society we find that cooking in paper or aluminium foil is more convenient than cooking in leaves, after all leaves don't grow on trees, or do they?

Pudding On The Agony
Pudding is a word that means different things under different circumstances. One meaning of pudding is a kind of sausage where meat or meat products with binders such as oats, bread or rice are stuffed into a skin. Examples are black pudding and haggis. Another type of pudding is, in effect, a cake which is boiled instead of baked. The third type of pudding is similar to a pie where a semi-liquid filling is enclosed in a pastry case and boiled. As I just explained, the only difference between suet dumplings and suet pastry is the way they're cooked. It's usual to use suet pastry for meat puddings and, since they are boiled, the pastry comes out the same as dumplings.

Puddings are generally more spherical than pies. They were

originally boiled in a cloth to hold everything together which
naturally formed into a ball shape. Now they are usually cooked
in a dish but it's typically much deeper than a pie dish. Puddings
are big, solid things, so it takes a long time for the heat from the
water to penetrate through to the middle of the pudding and
cook it. For a large pudding it can be several hours – it can even
take the best part of an hour just to reheat a pudding that has
already been cooked. Microwaves are especially good at cooking and reheating puddings because they put the heat deep under
the surface. If the pudding isn't too big the microwaves will heat
it all the way through in just a minute or two.

There's very little difference between a dumpling and a
pudding and, as with the word pudding, dumpling seems to have
more than one meaning. One kind of dumpling consists of
pastry, usually made with suet, cooked in a stew or soup.
Another kind of dumpling is a ball made of a cereal such as rice
or cracked wheat mixed with anything of appropriate size and
consistency such as minced meat, chopped fruit or chopped
vegetables. This kind of dumpling can have surprises in the
middle like large pieces of meat or fruit.

The last kind of dumpling that I could think of is the pasta
parcel where a sheet of pasta is wrapped around a typical pie
filling like minced meat or cheese. This is common in northern
China and something similar is found in Italian cookery. As
usual with the Italians, each shape has a special name. The best
known are ravioli, which are small cushion shapes, and cannel-
loni, which are fairly large tubes. The pasta has to be fresh or, if
it has been dried, it has to be cooked in water to soften it
otherwise it can't be used to make parcels. The Italians usually
finish off the preparation of these dishes by cooking them in an
oven with a sauce and lots of cheese.

Getting Laid

Putting things on top of other things is almost as popular as
putting things inside other things. When you start looking at it
an amazing number of food products are made in layers. The
idea is to have textures and flavours close together but still
keeping their own separate identity. Layers are usually of a solid
or very thick liquid consistency but we find layers so fascinating
that there are even examples of layered drinks. A layered drink
has a surprise effect in that the top layer is in contact with the

taste buds in your mouth and tongue but the lower layers, with their different tastes and textures, pass through the top layer and either mix or contrast with it.

Beers form layers automatically and the effect is strongest in dark stouts such as Guinness. Part of the attraction of drinking these beers is in waiting for the head to form and, in my experience, the longer the wait the better the pint. In beer the head rises to the top because it's made up of gas bubbles, wrapped in beer. This mixture is much less dense than the liquid beer so it floats to the top and stays there. It just happens that the foam on stout is quite stable and lasts most of the evening. The head on most other beers disappears much more quickly and is usually gone about half way through a pint.

It has been suggested that Irish coffee was invented to copy the appearance of these beers for people who don't like beer. In Irish coffee, cream is floated on top of the coffee and the coffee is drunk through the cream so you get a contrast between the cold of the cream and the heat of the coffee, the blandness of the cream and the strong taste of the coffee, the thick fatty consistency of the cream and the thin liquid consistency of the coffee.

The density of the coffee has to be carefully controlled to make sure the cream will float. Double cream floats easily on water but the coffee in Irish coffee has whiskey in it so its density is lowered to being close to that of cream. To stop the cream from sinking, the coffee is sweetened with sugar which brings the density back up again. The cream will mix with the coffee if it's stirred, so the accepted technique is to slide the cream gently on to the top of the coffee over the back of a spoon to stop it mixing. Another variant is cappuccino coffee in which the milk is frothed up by steam to make a foam which floats on top of the coffee. This foam is stable because the heat from the steam denatures the proteins in the milk and sticks the bubbles together.

There was a vogue for multi layered cocktails in the 1960s in which different brightly coloured liqueurs were floated on top of each other in the same glass. The densities of the liqueurs were quite close to each other so these concoctions took some skill to make: you had to pour the right liqueur, in the right order, with a very steady hand, to stop them from mixing. Appropriate liqueurs were sold in kits, with instructions, for a while but the vogue didn't last long – probably because the liqueurs were chosen for their density and contrasting colour rather than for their flavour and because the cocktail had to be drunk with a steady hand which is quite unsuitable for an alcoholic beverage.

Cakes and pastries are often made in layers. Plain sponge cake isn't very interesting and the simplest thing to do is to put a layer of something sweet and sticky in the middle. The something has to be of the right consistency: too thick and it won't spread, too thin and it will run out the side or soak into the cake too much. Typical fillings are jam or buttercream, and the buttercream may be flavoured with chocolate or fruit or something similar. Another layer can be put on top as icing and this can be the same stuff or something different for contrast. Chocolate on the outside and jam on the inside is a good combination.

Pastries are usually made up of layers of pastry, filling and icing, to the extent that they can be difficult to eat. It's almost impossible to eat a vanilla slice without making a terrible mess. A vanilla slice consists of layers of flaky pastry and confectioners' custard. The pastry is quite stiff and strong but the custard flows quite easily so, when you try to pick it up or cut into it, the pastry stays intact and the custard squishes out the sides all over your hands or onto the floor. Excellent party food.

The Swiss roll is an interesting variant on the layer cake, being a very thin layer cake rolled up into a cylinder. It was probably invented as a way of cooking a cake quickly because the thinner a thing is the quicker heat can penetrate through to the middle. A cake that thin is pretty unappetising (it doesn't give you much to get your teeth into) but when you roll it up you get a thick cake that also happens to look good. Because it looks good the same principle has been applied to savoury foods, called roulades because they're 'roulled' up. The cake is usually replaced with something with a lot of bread in it to give it the strength needed for the handling, and the filling can be anything – salmon or vegetable pastes are common. A roulade is tricky to roll up and you need to use a trick such as laying it on a cloth and using that to start the rolling process.

I've already mentioned layered stews such as Moussaka and Lancashire hot pot but there are other savoury dishes that are traditionally made in layers. A typical one is the Italian lasagne which is made from sheets of pasta interleaved with a tomato and meat sauce and topped with a layer of cheese. You can invent dishes like this yourself but remember that they can't be stirred so they have to be cooked on a low heat for a long time to let the heat get through to the middle. The layers have to be made of something that won't break up too easily in cooking but not so strong that it can't be eaten. Pasta is good, as is potato or aubergine.

Some foods are made up into layers just for show and it can be quite difficult to make them behave. A classic example is fruit jelly. The easy way to make fruit jelly is to mix the contents of a can of fruit with a block of fruit jelly made up with a small amount of water. The fruit floats, so if you turn out the jelly onto a plate the fruit is all at the bottom. By the way, gelatine only dissolves in hot water so the quickest way to dissolve the block of jelly is to put it in a glass bowl with just enough water to cover it and then microwave it on full power for one to two minutes. This has the advantage that you don't have to use lots of hot water to keep the temperature up, so you've got room to put in the fruit, and it cools down quicker in the fridge.

Anyway, the hard way to make fruit jelly is to place the fruit in neat layers. To do this you have to put some of the jelly in the mould and let it set, at least enough to support the weight of the fruit. You then place the fruit carefully on the jelly and pour in some more jelly. This second lot of jelly has to be partly set to stop the fruit from rising so you have to catch the exact moment when it's thick but still pourable. This kind of jelly is pure showmanship and doesn't taste any different from the easy version. A similar trick can be done with vegetables.

The trifle is about as complicated as you can get in making desserts. It's not difficult but it does bring together all sorts of different techniques and puts them in layers in one bowl. In the bottom we have bits of cake which have to be baked (even if you bought special trifle sponges from a shop somebody had to bake them), next we have fruit in jelly and on top is custard and maybe cream. All these are easy to get in shops now so it's just an assembly job but if you had to make everything from scratch it would be no trifling matter! In a trifle you need to control the amount of mixing between the layers and you do this by waiting for each layer to partially set before you pour on the next. This way you get some mingling of flavours but the layers still stay distinct. Some people pour the fruit and jelly onto the sponge cakes and let it set but I don't like the texture of cake in jelly. I prefer the cake soaked in fruit juice at the bottom and either no jelly at all or a separate layer of jelly above the cake. By the way, if a home made cake comes out too dry you can always use it in a trifle.

Street Food

You might have noticed that I left out some of the more obvious stuffed and layered dishes – that's because I think they fit better in this section. I promised myself that this book would say something about street food which I believe is a seriously neglected branch of the culinary art. Making food suitable for eating in the street puts considerable limitations on the cook and limitations always bring out the best in the skilled artist. Street food needs to be quick to cook but it must not deteriorate too much if it's kept warm; it needs to be substantial and tasty and, most of all, it needs to be easy to eat while walking along.

The archetypal street food is the sandwich, by which I mean anything with bread round it. Bread is the ideal food packaging material: it's strong, absorbent and, unlike paper towels which are also strong and absorbent, it tastes good. Sandwiches can have just about anything in them, the bread can be just about any shape and they can be hot, cold or warm. The important thing is that you can pick them up and eat them without a plate or a knife and fork or even chopsticks. I'm in the game of categorising and listing things so we'll break down sandwiches according to the type of bread and the way it's used.

In England the word sandwich implies two slices of bread from a white cut loaf with something like cold meat, cheese or jam in the middle. This is the basis of the classic office worker's lunch and it's either brought from home or bought in a shop. This sandwich has a distinguished history. The story goes that it's named after the 4th Earl of Sandwich who was around between 1718 and 1792. He was such an addicted gambler that he wouldn't leave the gaming table and during a marathon 24 hour session he was fed on cold beef in slices of toast. But the idea of combining food with bread was much older than that. In the middle ages plates, even wooden ones, were a luxury and a large piece of bread called a trencher was used instead. (When they could get a wooden plate they called that a trencher too.) The food would be eaten from the trencher and when the meal was finished the diner would eat the trencher. I imagine the trencher, soaked with meat juices and with bits of vegetables stuck to it, was probably the best part of the meal. Even today if you have kebab sitting at a table in a restaurant it will be served on top of bread although the bread itself will be on a china plate.

The basic white-bread-and-slice-of-meat type of sandwich has developed in recent years into an extravaganza of fancy breads and fancy fillings to try and entice the jaded palates of office workers. As well as the white bread there is now brown, wholemeal, granary and maybe, in the more adventurous places, rye. The bread may have other ingredients such as cheese and Mediterranean dried vegetables in it. The fillings all include salad and a rich, creamy dressing, such as mayonnaise or avocado, stacked high so that there's much more filling than bread. This type of sandwich is very popular but I find it a bit sickly. The flavours of all the fancy, expensive ingredients are lost in a sort of rich blandness, so they all taste the same and it doesn't really make any difference which filling you pick.

A sandwich is at its most nutritious, and I believe most satisfying and tasty, if there's much more bread than filling. As we'll find out in the bit on nutrition, a meal should be mostly carbohydrate with just a taste of fat and protein. These new trends in sandwiches turn that idea on its head with the bulk being fat and protein with just a trace of carbohydrate. Even the bread is so light and fluffy that it's almost all air. I like a sandwich made from a relatively heavy bread with some flavour, such as granary, and a simple filling that also has a strong flavour, such as mature cheddar.

The other development is the hot sandwich. This has an ancient history in the kebabs of Persia which I'll talk about in more detail in the section on world cooking. A more recent manifestation of the hot sandwich are burgers and hot dogs. These have swept the world, driven by American cultural imperialism (to use a heavy, politically charged phrase). I've got to sound off about burgers and hot dogs as well, especially burgers. I find both the bread and the meat flabby and tasteless, and the cucumber, onion, ketchup and other relishes are no substitute for the missing taste of meat and bread. Try making a burger for yourself from reasonable quality mince and good bread and you'll see what I mean. You don't need to use a bun, in fact a slice from a loaf works better.

The French have a snack called Croque Monsieur which is cheese and salami in a piece of baguette (the classic French bread). It's heated so that the cheese melts and the fat in the salami softens. If good ingredients are used this is an excellent meal but, if not, it can be greasy and grisly. The French also put stuff in other kinds of bread such as croissant and filled croissants are very fashionable in England at the moment.

My favourite hot sandwich is the kebab. I'm not fussy about which kind, I like them all. There's the doner kebab, which is that huge conical lump of meat that they cook on a vertical spit and take slices off, the shish or sheik which is mince pressed in a sausage shape around a skewer, or the tikka which is small lumps of meat threaded onto a skewer and marinaded in sauce. The sheik kebab is almost always made from lamb mince but the other kebabs are either lamb or chicken. The most common type of bread for kebabs is the pitta of Turkey and Greece which forms a convenient pocket inside as it's cooked. The pitta bread is slit along one edge and opened carefully. Filled with meat and salad it makes the classic street kebab.

If the kebab restaurateurs come from India, rather than Turkey or Greece, they will usually offer Nan bread instead of pitta. This is cooked fresh on the premises in a clay oven called a Tandoori and because of this has a better taste and texture than pitta which is usually baked elsewhere. Nan doesn't form a pocket like a pitta, so you can't put food inside it. You just roll it up a bit and eat it the best you can. This is where the concept of street food starts to fall down because a well stuffed sandwich or kebab is almost impossible to eat with your hands without bits falling out and sometimes a complete collapse. Some people are quite happy to leave a trail of lettuce, onion and bits of meat and to have chilli sauce up to their elbows but some, strangely enough, are not.

Street food can be better behaved. I think the neatest is another variant of the kebab called a Keema Nan. In this the meat of a sheik kebab is put in the middle of the uncooked dough of a nan which is then baked in the usual way. The result is a sandwich in which the filling is totally sealed in the bread and there's no leakage or fallout.

Toasted sandwiches are another way of keeping the fallout under control but you need special equipment to make them. This special equipment consists of two shaped plates which are hinged together and are either electrically heated or designed to be put on a stove. A piece of boring white bread is put on each plate, the filling is put between them and the sandwich maker is closed. Once the sandwich maker has cooked the sandwich, the top and bottom are sealed together so well that they can safely hold a liquid filling such as an egg or melted cheese. Of course the red hot filling squirts out as you bite into the sandwich and your mouth gets scalded, so you're living dangerously when you eat it!

A traditional loaf has a strong crust and a soft centre which makes it ideal for stuffing once the middle has been scooped out. I came across an example of this while working in the East End of London. The local school kids would use their dinner money to buy a small, crusty loaf of bread from a baker. Taking a half each they would walk along the street eating the soft bread from the middle. They timed this so that by the time the middle was empty they would be at the chip shop where they would get the loaf filled with chips to make an excellent chip butty. While I must abhor this practice on nutritional grounds I must admit it shows superb initiative and tastes very good. The principle is sound and it can be used for other fillings. As long as the filling isn't too wet the bread will keep its shape and you can play tricks by making it look like an ordinary loaf until it's cut open.

Sandwiches don't have to have lids. The Scandinavians never put tops on their smorgasbord but then they don't eat them in the street. Their bread is usually denser and less risen than the typical English white loaf and doesn't lend itself to the closed sandwich. The toppings of smorgasbord are much the same as the fillings of closed sandwiches but, as they are on view, they must look good too.

When it comes to hot open sandwiches the Italians have cornered the market with the pizza. That's all a pizza is – a hot open sandwich – but it has a mystique all of its own. Pizzas can have any topping but the most popular, by a long way, is some variation on cheese and tomato. As street food, a whole pizza is usually a bit too big but slices of pizza fit the bill perfectly. To make sure they don't miss out on anything the Italians also make a pizza with a lid, or rather a pizza that's been folded over. It's called a calzone and it usually contains a wetter filling than a pizza.

Next to bread the most convenient container for street food is pastry. Pies are often available as take away lunches, usually meat but sometimes fruit. They're so convenient that you can find them in all sorts of different food shops such as chippies, bakers and sometimes butchers. By the way, a pie from a butcher can often be the best as they put in lots of meat and the pastry is often home made.

The pasty is similar to the pie but a different shape and with a much more interesting history. The pasty is the traditional lunch of the Cornish tin miner of many years ago and its shape is entirely functional. The pastry is folded over the filling and the edge is turned over to form a seal. This turned over edge becomes a tasteless, uninteresting lump but its original function was to act as a handle for the miner to hold in his dirty hands. When he was finished he'd throw the thick strip of pastry away. The other gimmick is that the genuine pasty is a complete meal. The main filling is a thick meat stew with vegetables, and some enterprising wives used to put fruit or jam in one end as a dessert.

Various types of pancake can work as street food. The French serve crêpes filled with sweet or savoury fillings and the chip shops sell pancake rolls filled with vegetables and deep fried. The Mexicans are the greatest exponent of the filled pancake in the form of the taco which is a main part of the diet. Tacos are made from corn flour, as wheat doesn't grow well in Mexico, and they are either hard or soft. The soft taco has the texture of a pancake and can be used to wrap food in a neat package in the same way. The hard taco is like a large crisp and, while it looks nice filled with Chilli con Carne or refried beans, it's almost impossible to eat without it cracking and sending its contents all over the floor.

Speed is of the essence with street food and because of this it's often called fast food. A certain chain of hamburger restaurants made their (not inconsiderable) reputation on the speed with which they would supply you with your meal, often before you'd finished your order. There's nothing new about this, fish and chip shops had been doing it for years but hadn't made so much fuss about it.

Fish and chips is a strange choice for street food but in practice it works very well. Both the fish and the chips can be picked up in the fingers without falling to bits and it's not all that messy. Instead of a plate, the traditional wrapping for fish and chips has always been paper and, up until quite recently, it was always old newspaper which had just the right combination of strength and absorbency.

The fact that the ink came off the paper onto your hands and your food didn't seem to put people off back then.

The strangest street food of all is soup but that's the main lunch diet of the Far East. Obviously the soup needs a bowl, which the stall holder wants back, but it is sold in the street. The sustenance comes from noodles which are eaten with chopsticks and the soup is drunk from the bowl so there isn't too much washing up. The noodles are thin so they cook in a matter of seconds and the soup is heated ready to go so it certainly qualifies as fast food.

Making A Meal Of It

So far we've looked at cooking individual ingredients then at making up dishes and now we'll go to the next stage of complication and have a go at complete meals. The reason we eat meals is that we can't get enough variety from individual dishes although some dishes, especially the ones I just described as street food, are complete meals in themselves. It's easier to create interesting contrasts of taste and texture in a selection of dishes than to try to cram it all into one dish. The form that a meal takes is the most culturally defined of all our eating habits. The things that we eat and the way we prepare them are often controlled by practicalities based on what grows in the area and what cooking facilities we have, but the way we combine dishes into meals is different for different people.

There are two basic forms that a meal can take: it can be a help-yourself buffet or each person can be given their own plate with everything on it. Of course, it's not that simple and there are combinations of these two ideas. The everything-on-a-plate meal is very much the norm in northern Europe and North America but in most of the rest of the world some sort of buffet style is more usual. These two styles of presenting food are echoes of the grand banquets of the nobility which were an important way of showing off one's wealth.

A banquet can impress either by putting on a huge show at the table in one go, like the modern buffet, or by a seemingly endless succession of dishes on plates. Modern restaurant meals are imitations of these styles which is why a buffet has to be much bigger than is necessary to feed the number of people expected and why, as an absolute minimum, a meal has to have it's obligatory starter, main course and dessert. The grander the meal, the more courses we expect. We are so used to this cultural background that we expect a meal to take the form of courses even if it doesn't work very well. Other cultures don't eat this way and you can see the result in Indian and Chinese restaurants where starters and desserts are offered but they are not really integrated into the meal.

For about a hundred years home cooking has also tried to ape the style of the nobility although on a limited budget. This is a part of the obsession of the Victorian middle class to 'better themselves' which they did by imitating the upper class as well as they could. So, as well as having long complicated meals with many courses and altogether too much food, they placed the emphasis on the expensive part of the meal which was usually the meat. Outside of this tradition the emphasis is on the carbo-hydrate part of the meal – the bread or rice or whatever – and meat, if you can get it, is just flavouring. This is illustrated by the fact that the typical English meal is called 'meat and two veg', whereas in Japan 'taking rice' means eating a proper meal and in the Bible 'breaking bread' with someone meant eating a meal with them.

The idea of making meat the centre of the meal was strongly entrenched in northern Europe a long time ago but when the northern Europeans settled in America it became an obsession and changed the ecology of the whole continent. The land was turned over, almost entirely, to cattle and a significant propor-tion of the country's industry was, and still is, concerned with meat production. With this background it's no surprise that refusing to eat meat is considered to be a very strange action. Seen in this light it looks like choosing not to eat a proper meal, which is madness. It's like a Chinaman refusing to eat rice.

To design a meal you start with the main component and build up from there with a number of dishes as adjuncts to the main ingredient. If it's a northern European/North American meal you start by deciding what meat to have. Then you select the vegetables to go with it, then the starter, then the dessert and then, if you're really being flash, you decide on extra courses like a fish course after the starter or cheese after the dessert. On the other hand, if it's a meal from just about any other cultural tradition you start by choosing the carbohydrate – bread, rice, couscous etc. – then you select a few dishes to complement it. Some of these dishes will have meat in them and some won't, so it's an easy step to going entirely veggie – you just choose the dishes without meat. In the northern European culture there's no concept of a vegetarian meal because you haven't got the meat to build the meal around. This means that it's easiest to go to other styles of cooking, like Indian or Chinese, to make an acceptable vegetarian meal.

Meat is so important that it takes on ritual significance in grand meals like Sunday Lunch when the man of the house takes on the arduous duty of carving the roast even though he wouldn't be seen dead serving any other kind of food. In Morocco the centre piece of the meal is the carbohydrate in the form of a pile of couscous from which everyone helps themselves, whereas in Japan or China you're given your own bowl of rice and you help yourself to the accompanying dishes. Where bread is the bulk of the meal, as in Northern India and Persia, you usually get your own piece and help yourself to the other dishes. The rules of etiquette are different in detail in each culture but they aim to ensure that everyone has a fair share of food in both quantity and variety and that everyone gets a go at the best bits. The rules make sure that guests are suitably impressed as they are usually offered the good stuff before the hosts get any.

We're caught in a trap between our tradition of hospitality, which requires that we put out far more food than could possibly be needed, and our tradition of frugality, which requires that we don't waste anything. Because of this some people can't stop eating when there's food in front of them and they get fat. I know, I'm one of them. Think of this when you're catering; you'll probably find that most people will be grateful to be served with just the right quantity and are no longer impressed by excess. They also like to know what's coming next so they can 'pace themselves' to be able to finish the meal without overeating.

Some meals consist entirely of nibbles, although they're not usually reckoned to be meals at all, which can cause havoc with your waistline if you indulge in them too often. Nibbles are usually served under circumstances where the main activity is to drink a lot of alcohol, so they turn up at bars and cocktail parties. They're also used to keep people happy while they're waiting for their main meal so there's always the risk that the dinner guests will eat so much before the meal that they won't want any more. The sort of thing you'll find are small, bite size portions of tasty foods with lots of variety. Every country has its nibbles but they're different in different parts of the world. In Spain they're called Tapas, in Greece Meze, in Italy Antipasto, in France Hors d'Oeuvres, in Japan Sushi and in Indonesia Dim Sum.

The point I'm trying to make is that there's no set way of making a meal. What you're used to is quite alien to someone from another culture. You can experiment with the form of a meal just as you can experiment with the form of the dishes that make it up. Go for contrasts of flavour and texture, put hot spicy dishes with bland dishes, put dry or sticky dishes with ones with lots of wet sauce, put light dishes with heavy rich ones and combine them on the same plate or sequentially as separate courses, it doesn't matter. One thing you should do is to try to make your meal nutritionally balanced, as I'll explain in a later chapter. As well as making it healthy this will automatically make it a good balance of flavours and textures.

Time And Tide
One thing that gets some people into a total tizzy is timing – that is, making sure everything gets to the table at the right time and at the right temperature. The method for dealing with this is called planning and, while the principles are simple enough, it doesn't happen by itself. I'm going to talk about planning a meal but the ideas work for anything and I learned them during my work as a professional engineer. You'll probably find that you know all this already but I don't suppose you'll have done it as formally as this. The important thing is to think about what you're doing using some sort of structure, that way you're less likely to forget anything and get caught out.

For the planning to work you need to be clear about what you're aiming to do. You need to decide what you're going to make, how much of it and for when. If circumstances mean you can't be sure of how many people are going to turn up, or when, then you'll need some contingency plans. The first part of the plan is to make a list of all the steps you need to go through to get from where you are to where you want to be (planners call these steps Activities). The list can be in your head but if you start getting lost try writing things down. The easiest way is with a sort of bar chart where the lengths of the bars are proportional to the time taken for each step. The next thing is to guess the time it will take for each step and put the steps in order. The order the steps go in is usually pretty obvious when you start to think about it, but I'll give you an example to make it clear.

1. Decide what you're going to cook
2. Work out the ingredients you'll need
3. Check what you've already got in stock
4. Go to the shops and buy what you haven't got

Of course there are lots more steps before you reach the goal of feeding your guests. The trick with these steps is to break them down small enough so that you can give an accurate guess as to how long they'll take and so that they are in fact one activity and not a series of activities that might interfere with each other. However, if you do this you end up with an awful lot of steps and a very long list. The best way to deal with this is to look at the steps in groups so that, for example, the list above becomes 'Get the stuff' – but don't forget that it's really several steps in sequence.

As you're doing this you'll notice that some steps have to be in sequence (for example, you can't go shopping until you know what you want). On the other hand, some steps don't depend on what went before and can be started at any time. This means that you can have all sorts of things happening at the same time, which is where the planning gets interesting and can be a real help. I'll take the preparation of a typical meat and two veg meal as an example.

1. a Prepare meat
   b Cook meat
   c Carve meat
   d Serve meat

2. a Prepare vegetable 1
   b Cook vegetable 1
   c Drain vegetable 1
   d Serve vegetable 1

3. a Prepare vegetable 2
   b Cook vegetable 2
   c Mash vegetable 2
   d Serve vegetable 2

If you've ever cooked a meal like this you'll know where I'm heading. The aim is to get all the ingredients on the plate at the same time but we know that the cooking and preparation takes a different length of time for each one. Obviously you pick the one that takes the longest, say it's the meat, and start that first. While the meat's cooking you can start the next longest job, and so on, until everything is underway. Time the start of each sequence so that they all finish at the same moment.

Now you can see why you had to guess the length of time each step would take: it's so that you can put them in order of time. You can then sort out which sequence of steps is going to add up to the longest time. Planners call this longest sequence the 'Critical Path' and it's also the time the whole job will take because you can be doing everything else in parallel. To find out when you should start you work backwards from the time you need to be finished. You also work backwards from the end time to find out when you should start all the other sequences of steps.

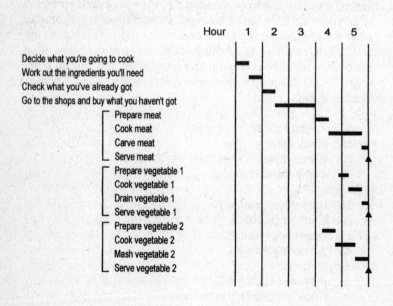

Fig. 14 Plan for cooking dinner

You can probably see the next problem coming up now: how are you going to do everything at once? This is the bit planners call resource management and it's all about finding ways to do a number of things at the same time. Here are a few examples of resources that you might run short of: the main one is people to do things, it might only be yourself; then there's cooking utensils and serving dishes; then cooking facilities, like enough rings on the cooker or space in the oven; and finally, there's space to put it all, especially worktops. If you really run out of resources then you have to change your plan because you won't be able to do the activities in parallel. This might not be a big problem, it just means the job will take longer and it's quite legitimate to trade a longer duration for less resources, but it does mean you have to start earlier. If you didn't do your planning properly then you'll only realise you haven't got enough time when it's already too late to start early enough. This is when panic sets in but there are still lots of things you can do to save the day.

The first thing you can do is to try and sort out some more resources. If people offer to help you can take them up on it but decide beforehand what you want them to do otherwise you'll waste your own valuable time getting them started. It's best to get your helpers to work in another room – setting the table or prettifying the hors d'oeuvres or something like that. That way you can all get on with your jobs without interfering with each other. Beg, borrow, steal or even buy, more cooking and serving dishes and maybe more cooking equipment such as a microwave and set up a table to give yourself more room. If all that doesn't work, think about what you're trying to make and see if you can streamline the process or if you can leave something out. For example, you can cook many different vegetables at the same time in the same container.

So how long will it take to cook dinner? Assuming you've done the shopping, and I strongly recommend you get that done long before you start, preferably the day before, you can get most meals done within an hour to an hour and a half. Food preparation usually takes less than half an hour and most food can be cooked within half an hour. Don't forget to get the defrosting started early enough if you use frozen food and remember to start pre heating the oven or boiling up cooking water while you're doing the preparation. The main thing that will make the process longer is if you have to cook something slowly because it's big, like a turkey or a joint of meat, but that should be on the critical path and you can get everything else done while it's cooking. There's often a balance between the cooking time and the preparation time so, for example, something that cooks very quickly, like a stir fry, takes a lot longer to prepare.

To Have And To Hold

If you haven't got the resources but you have left yourself enough time you still run into a problem: which is, that most food won't wait, it has to be eaten when it's ready and can't be left standing around. Your plans need to allow for this and you'll need to learn a few tricks to get it all to come together. Caterers are expert at this and they know which foods can wait around a bit and which ones can be finished off at the last moment. The difference between a good caterer and a bad one is just how expert they are at this. The best cooking can be ruined by being served at the wrong time whereas, if the timing is right, even the simplest dishes come out good.

There are three things you can do to keep food waiting: you can hold it at its serving temperature, you can keep it cold and heat it up to serving temperature when it's needed, or you can partly cook it and finish it off when it's needed. Holding food at serving temperature is fraught with problems. First there's the equipment needed to keep the temperature under control. If the food is served cold you keep it in the fridge or on ice but if the food is served hot you need a hotplate or a Bain Marie. These may be electrically heated but the traditional Bain Marie consists of a tank of hot water with containers for food suspended in the water. The high specific heat of the water keeps the temperature constant for a long time. The Hostess trolley is the domestic equivalent of the caterer's Bain Marie.

The food needs to be kept above 63°C because food poisoning bugs are reckoned to be killed at that temperature. If the temperature is less than that the bugs will multiply fast and anybody eating it will probably get ill. While this temperature keeps the food safe and at a pleasant temperature to eat, it has all sorts of other bad effects on the flavour and texture of the food. Moist food will dry rapidly at this temperature and many foods will form a skin on top as the surface dries out (this happens with sauces, gravy and custard). On the other hand, dry food will absorb moisture from the air and get soggy (this is worst with fried food such as fish and chips). Keeping the air out by putting the food in a box with a sealed lid or covering it in cling film will help to stop it drying out.

Of course, this temperature is high enough to continue some of the cooking processes which will tend to change the flavour of the food, usually for the worse. These effects limit the amount of time you can hold food and, although it depends on the food in question, a rule of thumb is about half an hour, tops.

Food that is served cold can be kept cold for quite a long time which is why caterers often have a cold starter already on the table for a sit down dinner. It's also why buffets usually consist mainly of cold salads. To keep the bugs down the temperature needs to be below 10°C so you can't leave it out on the table for long. Again, half an hour is about right. Things like ice cream, that have to be cold to keep the right consistency, won't survive long at room temperature and need to be served quickly.

Some cooked food can be stored cold and reheated at the last minute but it's very rare that it's as good as freshly cooked food. I expect that one of the reasons you're reading this book is that you want to cook for yourself instead of heating up convenience food. I've found that wet foods like soups and stews reheat very well and can even be improved by standing around for a day or so but anything dry can't stand that kind of treatment. Sauces thickened with flour are not at all happy about being reheated; they tend to curdle and separate and should be served fresh. Some of the additives in convenience food are to stop sauces from separating when they are reheated, you'll see them listed as 'stabilisers' or 'emulsifiers'.

You have to be careful about food poisoning if you cool and reheat food. The trick is to minimise the amount of time the food is between 10 and 63°C so you need to cool it down as quickly as you can for storage in the fridge and reheat it as quickly as you can when you want to eat it. Unfortunately, domestic fridges don't work too well if you put hot stuff in them so it's best to let the food cool down in a cold room first. A microwave is good for reheating as it's quick and it's less likely to dry food out but as with all microwave cooking you need to stir the food or there will be cold spots. If there's a large quantity try reheating separate portions in the microwave because the waves penetrate all the way into a small quantity whereas they won't go all the way through a large potful.

The other option is to finish off the cooking at the last minute, and this can be the most effective and dramatic thing to do, but it also takes considerable preparation and confidence. For a lot of food the actual cooking is very quick but the preparation can take a long time. The trick is to get everything ready and organised in advance and calmly do the cooking at the last minute. Do it in front of everybody if you've got the nerve. Have all the ingredients, and I mean all – even the salt and pepper – measured out and ready to hand, make sure everything is fully prepared and that you've enough space to put everything. You'll need the serving plates nearby, and somewhere to put them, and preferably a helper who knows what they're doing. If you want to look really good it's probably worth having a rehearsal and treat it like a theatre performance which, of course, it is.

You can use the Chinese style of cooking with a wok or you can deep fry or grill food quickly. Some of these techniques can be done at the table by your guests so you don't have to do any cooking at all, although you'll need some special equipment for cooking at the table. Examples are fondue, where everyone cooks up their food in melted cheese, or tempura, where the food is deep fried at the table. The barbecue is another example, where the cooking is done on demand in full view of the prospective eaters.

Some food can be partly cooked so that it only takes a few minutes to finish off. Vegetables can be done this way, especially potato chips. Part cooked bread can be finished off in the oven so that it comes out freshly cooked after a very short time. The storage rules about keeping the food above 63°C or below 10°C also apply to the uncooked or partly cooked ingredients, so be careful. Don't leave these ingredients hanging about for too long, either, or the results won't be any good even if it is freshly cooked.

All That Glisters Is Not Gold

I'm not very interested in presentation for its own sake, I think it's another leftover from the Victorians trying to imitate the nobility, but there's no doubt that the appearance of food has a big effect on how appetizing it is. Freshly cooked food made from fresh ingredients usually looks pretty good without any fancifying, and little frills or garnishes can be so trivial as to put people off. I like to see my food on clean, matching china plates and eat it with matching cutlery but even in this I might be being a bit Victorian. Obviously anything in contact with food needs to be clean but it doesn't have to be virginal white or perfectly formed and if you want to eat with your fingers then go for it.

The trend towards healthier food which has no added colouring and more fibre means that there's a strong possibility of 'Brown-out' where everything on the plate is the same wholemeal brown with no visual relief from other colours. You don't have to do anything about this, because you have the moral high ground, but if you're concerned about excessive brownness you could sprinkle on some appropriate naturally coloured ingredients such as pieces of red or green pepper or tomato. Choose serving dishes that contrast with the food and make sure they're the right size.

The relationship between the size of the dish and the amount of food served on it has a strong psychological effect. If the plate is almost covered and stacked high you'll feel you've had enough even if it's a small plate and there really isn't much on it. Within reason people don't notice how big the plate is, only how much it's covered by food, so if you want to appear generous use small plates. (You can use the trick in reverse to coax people to eat by putting a small amount on a large plate.)

It's worth putting some effort into the look of a plate of food or a loaded buffet table but don't forget that food is for eating not for looking at so don't go overboard. Simple things that don't take much extra effort are to slice food neatly and lay it on the plate in tidy patterns or to cut salad vegetables into fancy shapes. If these things come easily to you then do them but don't make a big deal out of it. People don't expect a big show these days but they do appreciate good food.

6

THE WONDERFUL WORLD OF WHEAT

WOW !!
Wheat flour is absolutely, totally amazing. It's so special that
there's an entire branch of cooking, called baking, devoted to
it. In the good old days the baker was the most important
person in the village and some of the earliest laws relate to the
purity and weight of bread. Wheat flour is the basis of pasta,
bread, pastry, biscuits and cake, so our diet would be pretty
thin without it.

You can't eat wheat, we humans aren't equipped to digest it,
so we've got to do things with it. I'm always amazed at the
complexity of the processes that the old men developed without
any scientific understanding of what they were doing – it just
goes to show that science isn't the only way of doing things.
Anyway, the first thing they did was give the wheat a good
bashing by grinding it between two stones which turned it into
the familiar flour.

At this point we lower our heads and muse on the idea that
the wheel is an invention to enable people to move around
whereas the millstone, which is the same size and shape, is an
invention which ensures that people stay in the same place.
Cool.

Once you've got the flour the job's not over because we
can't digest flour either. The next trick is to add water – now
we're cooking. Adding water to flour makes an interesting
paste or dough (depending on how wet it is). Now, at last,
we've got something we can cook and eat, and, depending on
what shape you make it, you've got pasta, semolina or unleavened bread.

What's Oop ~~Flour~~ Flower?

Flour is mostly starch with a bit of fibre (called bran) from the husk of the wheat seed. Starch is pure carbohydrate which is our main fuel supply and we now know that a bit of fibre is good for our internal workings, even if we don't digest it very well. There's also a tiny bit in each seed, called the germ, which is the baby wheat plant. This contains all sorts of good stuff: proteins, vitamins and minerals and, most important of all, taste. If you're not familiar with all this nutrition business I'll tell you about it later, meanwhile I'm still pretty excited about wheat.

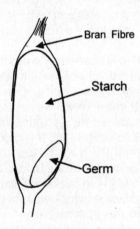

Bran Fibre

Starch

Germ

Fig. 15   A grain of wheat

Flour went down something of a nutritional blind alley. If grinding (or milling) is good then, they thought, more grinding must be better. The flour was milled more than once and each time it became finer and whiter because the bran and wheatgerm got left behind and thrown away. The result is a fine white powder, consisting almost entirely of starch, which is what we now know as white flour. Earlier cultures associated whiteness with purity and cleanliness, so white flour was sought after and associated with wealth and the high life. The same thing happened with sugar and rice. White flour, and the white bread made from it, is still with us, and it's still the biggest seller by a long way, but there has been a backlash. On the one hand nutritionists realised that we need the fibre in bran and the proteins and minerals in wheatgerm as part of our diet and on the other hand people who like food realised that factory made white bread is really boring and wanted something with taste and texture.

The result is that wholemeal flour, which is flour 'With nowt taken out', as one advertiser put it, is now freely available. Wholemeal flour has some bran and all the wheatgerm and, because it has been milled less, has a coarser texture than white flour. Not all brown flour is wholemeal, some brown flour is just white flour with brown colouring, so beware. When it comes to making bread nothing can give the light fluffy texture that you get from white flour but wholemeal flour makes a loaf with flavour and a solid consistency that means that it's real food to be taken seriously.

Bread making only works properly with wheat because wheat has the magic ingredient (gluten) which other cereals such as maize and millet do not. Rye has a bit of gluten but not enough to make the light, well risen bread we're used to. Gluten is a protein and proteins are nature's plastics, in other words they can turn from a liquid to a solid state if you do the right things to them. Gluten goes solid when it's heated so it's a sort of glue (gluten was named for its glueiness). In fact, flour and water can be used as a glue. Gluten is so important that we actually select our flour according to how much gluten is in it even though most of us don't even know that gluten exists.

The key word, at least in England, is 'Strong'. Strong flour has a high gluten content and is good for making bread, anything else has a lower gluten content and is good for cakes and pastry and stuff. Outside England you'll have to look carefully at the packet to see if the contents are recommended for bread making. You can find strong versions of white flour, brown flour and wholemeal flour. If the packet doesn't say anything about bread making it's safe to assume that the flour has a low gluten content; you can still make bread with it but it won't rise so well. The only thing you won't find is strong self-raising flour; that would be silly. Self-raising flour has baking powder in it (I'll explain what baking powder is soon, just wait a while, OK?) and you don't make bread with baking powder (unless you feel like it – rules are made to be broken).

In the quest to make bread with a bit more flavour two specialist flours have been developed: wheatmeal is brown flour with some wheat germ put back after milling, and granary is brown flour with malted wheat flakes added. Malting is a process where the grains of wheat are allowed to sprout and it gives a pleasant nutty taste to the bread made with it.

The wheat with the highest gluten content is called durum and it's used to make pasta because pasta is entirely stuck together with gluten. Flour made from durum wheat is called semolina.

The table summarises the various types of flour you can buy. Don't take the 'Use' column too seriously. You can use any flour for any purpose, it's just that some give better results than others.

Types Of Wheat Flour				
Usual Name	Alternative Name	Description	Gluten Content	Use
White	Plain, Cake	Highly refined	Low	Cakes, Pastry, Biscuits, Scones
Self-Raising		White flour with added Baking Powder	Low	Cakes, Scones
Strong White	Bread	Highly refined	High	Bread
Brown		White flour with colour and some wholemeal	Low	Pastry, bread
Strong Brown	Brown Bread	White flour with colour and some wholemeal	High	Bread
Wholemeal	Wholewheat	Less refined, retains all wheat-germ and bran	Low	Pastry, bread
Strong Wholemeal	Wholemeal Bread	Less refined, retains all wheatgerm and bran	High	Bread
Wheatmeal	Germ Meal	Brown flour with added wheatgerm	Low	Pastry, bread

| Granary | Brown flour with added malted wheat | Low | Bread |
| Semolina | Made from durum wheat | Very high | Pasta, Couscous |

Forever Blowing Bubbles

I reckon that some time in distant history, a few thousand years ago, somebody had some of this flour and water dough ready to cook and something happened – maybe the fire went out, or the hunter came home – and it was a few hours before they were ready to cook. On some of these occasions something strange would have happened to the dough, it would have increased in size quite a lot. Now either these people thought, 'Great! Now we've got more!' or, 'That looks weird but I'm hungry I'll cook it anyway.' Whatever they thought, they put the expanded dough on the fire and cooked it. Thus, I suggest, was bread invented and because it's so good to eat they made it that way every time from then on. This bread was such an attractive food that civilisation and agriculture were invented just so that we could have a regular supply of it.

What had happened is that something had blown gas into the dough which then set during cooking to make the familiar bread texture. The thing is, if you blow bubbles in a liquid and that liquid turns solid, you've got a foam and boy! do we like foams! We like foam so much that one of the most popular fillings for chocolate is air. Think of Milky Way, Aero, Wispa, Flake and Maltesers (with the 'Less fattening centre' – you can't get much less fattening than air!). Imagine the scene: the boardroom of a massive sweety factory, the chairman speaks:

'We need a filling for this new chocolate bar. Any ideas?'
'How about air?'
'Ridiculous! We can't sell air. Who'd buy it?'
'Well it is cheap.'
'OK, let's give it a go.'

We go to great lengths to get air into food when making cake, soufflé and meringue. Baking is mostly the art of getting these foams to behave themselves although there's a fair amount of baking where the result stays flat, such as biscuits and crackers.

So, we've got the structure of bread from the gluten and

starch but where do the bubbles come from? In the old men's bread the bubble blowing came by accident. Various yeasts, fungus and bacteria are floating around all the time. Usually these will spoil food but sometimes they improve it. Once a beneficial bug had landed on the dough the old men (or probably old women now I come to think about it) would keep that strain going by keeping a bit of infected dough to raise the next loaf. This kind of bread is called 'sour dough' and it tastes pretty good. The bugs in the dough are living, reproducing and, most important, breathing. Just like us they breathe in oxygen from the air and breathe out carbon dioxide, and it's this carbon dioxide gas that makes the bubbles. To get a good supply of bubbles you've got to look after the bugs. They need food, in the form of sugar, damp and warmth; too cold and they won't grow, too hot and they die.

After many hundreds of years of using the sour dough method, the use of yeast was introduced. Yeast is the name of many varieties of simple, plant like creatures which produce alcohol and carbon dioxide. Yeast is called a plant but it's so simple, being single celled, that it's not much different from a single celled animal or bacterium. I call them all bugs, it's easier. Yes, I said alcohol back there and the yeast used in brewing booze is much the same as the one used for bread.

Brewing and bread making are as ancient as each other but tend to have been kept separate because the knowledge of brewers and bakers was jealously guarded by their respective trade associations or guilds. You can use brewer's yeast to make bread or baker's yeast to brew beer but it's best to use the right one for the job because the strains have been optimised over hundreds of years to give the best results. For baking, the aim is to make lots of gas and not much alcohol; for brewing, of course, it's the other way round. The small amount of alcohol that's produced during bread making just evaporates away during cooking.

Yeast is very well behaved. As I said before, it needs warmth, dampness and food to reproduce but if it doesn't get any of those it doesn't die but has clever survival strategies. If it's too cold the yeast simply shuts down and doesn't do much at all and you can store lumps of it this way for days in the fridge. If yeast gets dry it goes into survival mode and forms itself into spores which are little round, hard pellets which are really tough. Yeast can be bought in this form and it works very well.

The other way to make bubbles is by a chemical reaction using sodium bicarbonate (or bicarbonate of soda, which is the old fashioned way of saying the same thing). This can be bought on its own or as baking powder where it's the main ingredient. When it gets wet, and some acid is added, sodium bicarbonate generates lots of carbon dioxide – that's the fizz in sherbet powder. Baking powder includes some acid in powder form, so you don't have to add any, but for some baking, such as scones, the acid is added in the form of cream of tartar (potassium tartrate). In some recipes the acid comes from another source such as vinegar, sour milk or lemon juice.

Traditionally yeast is used to raise bread and baking powder to raise cakes but, just to be perverse, you can make soda bread with baking powder and you can make cakes with yeast (Kugelhopf is a good example). The main difference is that baking powder starts making gas immediately, and blows it all out in a short period, while yeast takes a while to get going but then doesn't stop until it's killed off by the heat of cooking.

Making An Honest Crust

Bread is just flour, mixed with water and blown up with gas, so why is there so much mystique about making it? There are two problems. One I've already talked about is that yeast is alive and has to be looked after; the other is that the gluten is shy and doesn't want to come out to play. Yeast needs water, warmth and food so we start our bread making by getting the yeast in the right mood. Put it in some warm, sugary water (soft lights and smoochy music might also help but I've always managed without). If you leave this for about ten to fifteen minutes you should see a thick foam on the water. This is the sign that the yeast is doing its stuff and has been merrily bonking away making more yeast and lots of carbon dioxide.

Now, what was all that about gluten being shy? Well, the proteins that make up gluten are tightly bound up with the starch and they need quite a hammering to separate them out and get them to work. This is the purpose of kneading. The important part of kneading is the tearing action which breaks up the fabric of the dough and brings out the gluten. You can tell when it's working because the dough starts to feel elastic and stops being sticky. It's probably kneading that causes the problems when people try bread making. To do it properly you have to be a bit psychotic and rip the living daylights out of the dough. I never had any problems because I'm built like a brick outhouse but I've spoken to lots of people, mostly women, who've had problems making bread. All I can say, when it comes to kneading, is: 'Give it hell!!'. Remember, in a medieval village there were two guys you didn't pick a fight with: one was the blacksmith, the other was the baker.

So, you've got a dough with all the gluten working and full of happy yeast. What now? Walk off and leave it, that's what. The yeast will blow up the dough and the elasticity of the gluten will make sure it forms a strong foam. After an hour or so, depending on the humidity and the temperature, the dough will be about twice its original size and you knock it down with a bit of kneading and let it rise again. I don't know why you do this but everyone does, so why should I argue? When the dough has blown up again you knock it back again and put it in your baking tin where it's left to rise again. When it's risen enough to look like a loaf of bread you cook it. If you're in a hurry you can miss out one or maybe both of those rising sessions and you'll still get bread.

So now we've seen that the absolute minimum you need to make bread is flour and water but it's usual to add a few other things too. I've mentioned the yeast and the sugar that's needed to feed it. You'll also need some salt because bread is very unpleasant without it. It's quite usual to add some fat as butter or margarine to improve the taste, texture and keeping ability of the bread and adding milk will soften the crust and give white bread more flavour. None of these is essential to making bread, they are just embellishments.

Mister Pastry

Bread and pasta make a good healthy diet but humans are omnivores (that means we can and do eat anything and everything) so we're always looking for something different and we had to make baking more complicated. Two ingredients were added to flour to open up the field; these were fat and sugar. They have different effects and I'll take them in turn.

Fat is very important in the history of food. Just as wheat is an important supplier of energy but we can't eat it without processing it, so fat in its various forms is the most concentrated source of energy but it tastes horrible on its own. The simplest way to combine fat and starch is to spread it on bread as butter, margarine, dripping or even olive oil. The complicated way is to make pastry, pancakes, doughnuts, dumplings or batter. These are all pretty much the same: flour, fat and liquid (water or milk) are mixed together into a paste and cooked. If there's a lot of liquid it's a batter which you can pour into a frying pan to make a pancake, coat something with (fish for example) and deep fry it or bake to make Yorkshire pudding. If there's only a small amount of liquid you end up with a pastry dough which you can roll out and use to make pies or you can boil to make dumplings.

It doesn't really matter what fat you use but, in general, you need to use hard fats for baking (liquid oils don't usually give good results). The hard fats include margarine, butter, lard, suet and vegetable fat. Butter has a distinctive flavour of its own. By all means use it if you like that flavour, but marge is just as good and much cheaper! You can mix the different fats to give a particular flavour or consistency. Don't use the special easy spreading margarine, or other butter substitutes, because they don't work as well and they are more expensive than plain cooking marge. You also shouldn't use low fat spreads. These are made low fat by replacing up to half the fat with water and they break down when heated so they won't make good cakes or biscuits and, even if they did, the results wouldn't be low fat. The best candidate for making low fat cakes and desserts is cottage cheese. It isn't a direct replacement for fat but it's worth experimenting with.

There are two sorts of pastry: one with a lot of fat and one with a hell of a lot of fat. Short crust pastry is one part fat to two parts flour, by weight, but puff pastry has twice as much fat, in other words equal weights of fat and flour. By the way, 'short' means crumbly when talking about food.

Short crust pastry is easy to make: mix the flour with the fat and add water. Those are the basics but there are ways to go wrong. In many ways making short crust pastry is the opposite of making bread because the aim is to prevent too much gluten developing. Gluten is so strong that it would make the pastry tough and chewy. Use a low gluten flour and a hard fat such as butter, margarine or lard, or a mixture of these. Don't use modern spreadable margarine or butter or low fat spreads; soft fats or oil make a tough pastry. Mix the fat with the flour using your fingers. This stops you from kneading the dough, which would bring out the gluten, and you won't warm up the fat with the heat from your hands. The fat coats the flour grains which stops the gluten from sticking everything together. You should do all this with everything cool to keep the fat hard. You'll know the flour is mixed with the fat because it takes on an even consistency like breadcrumbs. Add a little bit of water (it always surprises me how little) and mix it in to make a dough. Be gentle because we are trying not to knead it. I find it's easiest to use a table knife and to mix the dough with a cutting action. You can tell when there's enough water because the dough forms up into a ball and doesn't stick to the bowl. If you overdo it, and the dough turns to goop, mix in some more flour. That's it, you've made pastry. If you're in a hurry you can roll it out straight away to make your pies, or whatever, but it's best if you leave it alone for a while. It's just been through a traumatic experience and it needs to relax.

On the theory that if some fat is good more fat must be better, somebody invented puff pastry. If you try to add more fat using the short crust method it simply doesn't work, there's not enough flour to soak up the fat. If you're very careful you can make a richer short pastry. I was shown a method using ten ounces of butter and two eggs to a pound of flour but it was a right old performance getting it to mix. The trick is to make a wall of the flour. In the middle you put the soft butter mixed with the eggs so you can pull the flour into this goop without letting it escape. If you want even more fat then you have to use another trick to get it to mix. You start off by making a dough with either just water or part of the fat and you roll this dough out flat. Then put the raw lumps of fat on top of the rolled out pastry, fold the pastry over it and roll the sandwich flat again. The fat is trapped in the dough and can't go anywhere even if it isn't happy about mixing with its less rich neighbours. To spread the fat out so that it isn't left in a lump in the middle, the folding and rolling is repeated a few times (six 'turns' is the recommended number). The result is puff pastry. Flaky pastry is similar. Amazingly enough, when you cook this stuff steam blows it up into the familiar flaky, crisp layers, so we've found another way of inflating our food.

Don't forget that nothing I've said is set in stone. If you get away with being heavy handed with your pastry, or if you use liquid paraffin instead of butter, or if you work in a warm room, then so be it. But, if everything always goes wrong, try some of these recommendations, they might solve your problems.

Naughty, But Nice

We've done fat, now let's look at sugar. If you add sugar to pastry you've got a biscuit, it's as simple as that. However, now we've got three ingredients so we can try something else. Instead of mixing the fat with the flour we can mix it with the sugar. This is called creaming and the sugar dissolves in the fat to form a mixture which is almost white in colour (even if you use a highly coloured fat, like butter). This is hard work and it's well worth while using an electric mixer. The interesting thing is that the sugar dissolves even though the fat remains solid. It doesn't really matter which method you use but here's a rule of thumb: use creaming when the combined weight of the fat and sugar is more than the weight of flour, otherwise rub the flour into the fat and add the sugar afterwards. If you use self-raising flour or add a bit of baking powder the biscuits will fluff up and have a lighter texture (this doesn't do your plain pastry any harm either).

A while back I was going on about how we like air in our food. Well, an inflated biscuit is a cake. You can use either of the methods above for making cakes and choose them for the same reason: use the creaming method for rich cakes and the rubbing in method for less rich. By the way, 'rich' is code for fatty. Making cake is a battle against gravity. Unlike bread, the matrix (that's a posh word for the stuff holding the bubbles together) isn't strong and there's only a limited amount of gas to do the blowing so we have to get up to a few tricks. The main thing is to get air into the mixture and keep it there. When we cream the sugar and fat we keep going until it gets fluffy and when we mix in the flour we do it gently to avoid knocking the air out. The cooking is critical. The oven has to be hot enough to solidify all the ingredients just at the time that the baking powder has had its effect. But if it's too hot the outside will bake hard and the inside will collapse. You can cook a thin, light weight cake quickly at a relatively high temperature – say, half an hour at gas mark 6 (400°F,

200°C) – but a large, heavy cake needs to be cooked much longer at a lower temperature, maybe as much as three hours at gas mark 2 (300°F, 150°C).

So far I haven't mentioned eggs because they make life much more complicated. However, you really need eggs to make cakes. Of course, you can make a cake without eggs but it's not very interesting. Like wheat, eggs are one of nature's little wonders. Eggs consist of two parts: the white and the yolk. (I know you knew that but I had to say it because it's important.) Both parts are mostly water with some protein but the yolk also has a fair proportion of fat (strictly speaking it's called lipid but it's enough like fat for our purposes). The egg protein can do the same job as gluten: you can blow bubbles in it and then set the bubbles into a foam by heat. In fact egg protein blows better foams than gluten which is why we take all the trouble to stop the gluten developing and use eggs instead. You get the foam started by beating the eggs which mechanically mixes in air.

This is about as complicated as it gets – we've got four ingredients and we have to decide on the relative proportions and the method of mixing them together. The first guess is to use the same quantity of each ingredient. Fortunately this works fine and it's called a Victoria sponge. The accepted method is to cream together the fat and sugar then beat in the eggs (one at a time to keep the air in) and, finally, add the flour. It's worth sifting the flour to get rid of the little round lumps which won't go away and will spoil the finished cake. At this point you may need to add some water because you want the mixture to be spreadable so that it fills the baking tin.

The Victoria sponge has about the lowest proportion of flour to other ingredients but you can make very successful cakes with a much higher proportion of flour. Usually the other ingredients are in about equal quantities. You can also add a fair weight of dried fruit, up to half as much as the other ingredients together. You can miss out the eggs or you can miss out the fat and you'll still end up with a cake.

Now that electric mixers are in most homes it's possible to ignore all these complex methods and just chuck all the ingredients in a bowl and mix like mad. An electric mixer has the power and the patience to get air into the relatively heavy mixture and a perfectly good cake can be made this way.

Loose Ends

The four ingredients – flour, fat, sugar and eggs – cover all the basics of baking but just about every combination of those ingredients has been tried out.

Flour on its own, as we have already seen, makes pasta and unleavened bread such as matzo or water biscuits. If it's blown up with gas from yeast or baking powder we get bread. If we add fat to the flour we get pastry. The more fat we add the puffier the pastry becomes and the more difficult it is to make. Dumplings are the same as pastry but it's usual to use suet as the fat. (Suet is a particular bit of fat that you find attached to animals' kidneys which is probably why they invented vegetable suet.) Adding sugar we get to biscuits and if biscuits are blown up we call them cakes.

All of these can have eggs added to improve them ('rich' usually means more eggs as well as more fat). Pasta all'uovo is pasta made with eggs and it's reckoned to be the best. Fancy breads often have eggs in them (a good example is brioche). Most biscuits and cakes include eggs, in fact the only cake that doesn't have eggs in it is called an eggless cake. Choux pastry has relatively little fat but has a lot of egg so it expands easily. This kind of pastry is cooked in small lumps or sausage shapes and it blows up to be fluffy with a hollow centre. The lumps are made into profiteroles and the sausages into éclairs.

Although I've gone along with the strict labelling of bread, biscuit, cake, etc., it's really a continuum where you add a bit of sugar and some egg to bread and it gets more and more cakey until you call it a yeast cake. Or you make your biscuits lighter and lighter until they might as well be cakes. Scones, brioche, teacakes and such sit in this middle ground between bread and cake.

The table summarises what I've just said about mixing flour with fat and sugar:

	Flat	Raised
Flour	Pasta, Water biscuit	Bread
Flour and Fat	Pastry	Puff Pastry
Flour and Fat and Sugar	Biscuits	Cake

The importance of flour, sugar, fat and egg set me thinking about what other combinations they were found in. Here are the ones I could think of:

Fat (oil) and Egg (yolk)	Mayonnaise
Sugar and Egg (white)	Meringue
Sugar and Egg (yolk)	Custard
Sugar and Fat	Buttercream Icing

The Plot Thickens

As we've seen, biscuits, cakes and pastries don't need gluten to hold them together, that's done by the eggs and fat. All they need is starch and you can get starch from all sorts of bits of all sorts of plants. Plants use carbohydrates in the form of starch or sugar to store energy. Starch is the more common form although sugar is found in sugar cane and sugar beet. Plants also use sugar in fruit and nectar to attract animals, birds and insects who, in turn, distribute the pollen or seeds of the plants. Seeds are plant babies and they come in a range of sizes from the tiny mustard seed to coconuts (nuts and seeds are pretty much the same thing). The bulk of each seed is made up of starch which acts as fuel for the baby plant to grow until it's able to use sunlight, soil and water to feed itself.

Seeds are the result of plants reproducing sexually (that is, when the daddy plant's pollen fertilises the mummy plant's ovule). Some plants don't use sex to reproduce. Instead they make exact copies of themselves by growing new shoots from the roots of an existing plant. Sometimes the roots lie in the ground waiting for good growing conditions and these roots also include large amounts of carbohydrate as an energy store for the new plant.

Whenever starch is ground up finely it's called flour which is why there's a bewildering array of different flours available all made from different plants. Most flour comes from cereals which are the seeds of grass-like plants but some comes from starchy root vegetables, peas, nuts or even pith. The table overleaf lists all the ones I could find; there may well be others.

Cereals: Seeds of Grass-like Plants	Wheat, Corn, Barley, Millet, Oats, Rice, Rye, Sorghum	
Roots and tubers of starchy vegetables	Potato	Flour is called Farina
	Cassava	Also called Manioc, flour is called Farina and prepared root is called Tapioca
	Arrowroot	Exceptionally pure, used to make clear sauces
	Kudzu	Native of Japan
Seeds of Rhubarb-like plant	Buckwheat	
Peas	Chana Dahl	Flour is called Besan
	Chick Pea	
Nuts	Chestnut, Hazelnut	
Pith of a Palm tree	Sago	

There's a reason for me waffling on like this about starch and flour. The main use for starch, apart from baking, is in thickening sauces. When starch is mixed with water and heated gently it absorbs the water and holds it together in a thick paste (techies call it a Gel). The reason that there are so many flours is that wheat flour isn't the best thickening agent. Wheat flour has a flavour of its own and tends to make clear liquids cloudy. If the sauce has strong flavours and is opaque then wheat flour is perfectly acceptable but, if not, then some other source of starch must be used. Typically corn or potato flour are used where the flavour is a problem, as in custards which are sweet sauces, and arrowroot flour is used where a transparent result is wanted. A small amount of starch will thicken a lot of water so it can be tricky to get the quantity right and lumpiness is caused by a local high concentration of starch. Lumps in sauces usually succumb to vigorous stirring so they are not really a big problem as long as you catch them in time.

7

YOU ARE WHAT YOU EAT

The Pre Prologue
If this is a book about cookery why should I go on about nutrition? Well, the politically correct reason is that everyone should understand nutrition so that they can eat a proper balanced diet and live long and prosper. But I believe that a diet that fits in with accepted nutritional principles also happens to be the most satisfying. Many thousands of years of evolution have fine tuned our appetites to match our nutritional requirements, so if we fancy something it's probably what we need. Unfortunately evolution hasn't caught up with the fact that it now takes very little physical effort for us to get food. This means that, when it comes to choosing food for energy, we tend to overdo it. When we were hunter gatherers, as some people still are, we would choose the highest energy foods we could find and store them in our bodies, as fat, until such time as it was difficult to get food. This is why we eat more than we need and because, for most of us, the lean times never come, we stay fat.

The connection between health and food has always been subject to fads and muddled thinking. It's possible that the ancient Jewish taboo against eating pork and various other foods had a basis in health precautions but, if it did, the reasons are long forgotten. Likewise the crusades for a particular diet have taken on the strength of an evangelical religion many times in the distant and more recent past. When the science of nutrition was young it was believed that protein was the most important thing and that meat should be the basis of all meals. This was taught with evangelistic zeal in American schools and, to a lesser extent, in Britain. The more recent trend to less (or no) meat and more carbohydrate and fibre also became something of a religion, if only to enable it to fight against the entrenched pro-meat lobby. Woody Allen summed it up in his film *The Sleeper*. The hero is a character who runs a macrobiotic (that is, strictly vegetarian) food shop in the early 1970s when such a thing was very fashionable but not at all mainstream. He falls asleep to awaken many years in his future. When he finds a health food restaurant, up there in the future, it only serves steak and chips! I hope that what I'm going to say isn't yet another fad but it does seem to be based on reasonably good science so I'll stand by it for the moment. Ask me again in two hundred years.

Now, let's take a quick look at what food is made of and what effect it has on us so that you can understand what's going on and make sensible decisions about what you're cooking and eating.

The Prologue

You are made out of chemicals and so am I. In fact, everything is made out of chemicals. Chemical is just another name for matter. So, you ask, what is a chemical? Well it's a long story but I'll try and whiz it along as fast as I can.

We've known for hundreds of years that some stuff changes when it's heated and that some substances change their form when they are mixed together. For a long time the alchemists thought that if you fiddled about mixing things and heating things you might be able to do something useful like make gold or live forever. Eventually they found that it didn't work like that and they invented modern chemistry. Modern chemistry goes like this:

All the millions of different substances are made up of combinations of only about a hundred different elements and each element has a unique atom. You can't break atoms any further using heat or mixing things together. But, using the higher energies that you find in atomic physics, you can get inside an atom. Then you'll see that it's made up of a heavy lump in the middle with lots of tiny things whizzing around it. The heavy lump is the nucleus, which is made of protons and neutrons, and the whizzy things are electrons.

Atoms are really, seriously small. You get about 600,000,000,000,000,000,000,000 of the smallest ones in a gram (that's six followed by twenty-three noughts) and nearly all the weight is in the nucleus. Electrons are even smaller – it takes nearly 2,000 of them to equal the weight of one proton or neutron (protons and neutrons weigh about the same).

As far as chemistry is concerned the important thing is electrical charge – that's the same electricity that lights your house. Don't worry what the protons, neutrons and electrons are made of and don't worry about what electrical charge and mass really are, these are problems that are taxing the minds of the greatest scientists in the world right now and even if they do come up with an answer don't expect it to make much sense in terms of our everyday world. Just accept that protons and neutrons have mass and that each proton has a positive electrical charge and each electron has an exactly equal negative charge. Positive and negative charges attract each other very strongly and like charges repel each other equally strongly.

There's a lot of dynamic tension in an atom: the electrons are all repelling each other and whizzing about like crazy but they're held in place by the attraction of the protons; the protons are all bundled up tight in the nucleus so they're repelling each other and trying to blow the nucleus apart. The things that stop the nucleus coming apart are the neutrons. Neutrons have no electric charge but they do have another similar property, called the strong nuclear force, which is enough to overcome the electrical repulsion of the protons and hold the nucleus together. The strong nuclear force only works over a short distance so it doesn't interfere with the electrons or any other nearby atoms. Chemistry is all about the interaction between the electrons of different atoms so the presence of neutrons makes no difference to chemistry.

The thing that makes an element unique is the number of protons in the nucleus. It's so important that it's called the atomic number and there's an element for each atomic number. Number 92 is uranium and that's the heaviest naturally occurring element. The heavier ones are man made and the heavier they get the more difficult they are to make and the faster they break down when they are made. So far we've got to 109 and there are probably more.

If you put the elements in order of their atomic number something very interesting happens, you get patterns where every eighth element is similar. Nowadays this is usually laid out as a table and called 'The Periodic Table of Elements'. It's very important because the pattern reveals something fundamental about the structure of atoms.

It turns out that the electrons don't just fly around any old how but arrange themselves in layers and there's a limit to how many electrons you can get in each layer. The innermost layer has a limit of two, so Helium (number two) has a full layer. The next layers can each hold eight electrons and it's the number of electrons in the outer layer that decides the chemical characteristics of an element. As the elements get heavier, things get more complicated and elements start to squeeze in between the second and third columns of the table but the pattern of eight is still there.

Atoms really, really want to get that outer layer filled up and that's why they do chemical reactions. Atoms at the left hand end of the table have a small number of electrons so they try to get rid of them to get to a full layer. Atoms at the right hand end already have a full layer so they aren't bothered about chemistry but the next ones in, in the seventh column, need an electron to fill up their outer layer.

So, counting from the left, atoms in the first column want to get rid of one electron, atoms in the second column want to get rid of two and in the third column three. Meanwhile atoms in the seventh column want to grab one electron, atoms in the sixth column want two electrons and in the fifth column three. The fourth column is in the middle: atoms in it can either accept or donate four electrons. These spare electrons, or the spaces where electrons want to be, act like hooks and enable atoms to hold onto each other. If you want to keep up with your scientist friends at a cocktail party then you should know that the number of hooks an atom has available is called its valency.

In order to get this outer layer filled, atoms combine with each other to form molecules. Molecules can all be the same atoms, for example a hydrogen molecule has two atoms stuck together, but it's much more interesting when different atoms stick together. Water is a good example. Oxygen needs two electrons to fill its outer layer and hydrogen wants to donate one. So two hydrogen atoms get together with one oxygen atom and the result is a stable molecule.

These combinations of atoms are called compounds and they are nothing like the elements that made them. The best example of this is common table salt. This is a compound of sodium and chlorine. We're all familiar with salt, it's pretty harmless: it doesn't explode or burst into flames or poison anybody. Sodium, on the other hand, is very nasty: it's so keen to react that it almost explodes if you put it in water. Chlorine is also very nasty: it's a poisonous, greenish gas that smells bad.

Carbon is special because it has four hooks waiting to grab other atoms, including other carbon atoms. It can form very complicated molecules because the carbon atoms can link together in chains and still have some electrons left over to hook on to other atoms. There are so many compounds with carbon in them that the study of carbon compounds has its own special name. It's called organic chemistry because most of the carbon compounds are found in living things. The study of everything else is called inorganic chemistry.

Eat To Live

We are machines for turning chemicals into us and copies of us. We get all the chemicals we need from our food and from nothing else. We use our food in two different ways: for fuel and for repair and building work. In fact we are made up of the same stuff as our food to the extent that, if we were really unlucky, we could be eaten as food ourselves. Any food can be used as fuel to give us energy and almost any food can be remodelled into stuff that we can repair ourselves with or use to grow bigger or make babies. Some foods are better at one thing than another and some foods have essential ingredients that we can only get from that kind of food.

All food is organic, as far as chemists are concerned, meaning that it's made up of carbon compounds. Food is mostly large molecules with long chains of carbon atoms. Each carbon atom has four hooks to play with. If it's in the middle of a chain it's using up two hooks, one for each of the neighbouring carbon atoms, so it's got two left over. These leftover hooks can connect with all sorts of atoms but the simplest, and most common, atom is hydrogen and that's the one that's used the most. Usually carbon atoms connect together with one hook but sometimes they use two. This double bond is less stable than the more usual single one. A compound with a double bond in it is more reactive because one half of the double bond can open up leaving hooks for other atoms to latch on to.

Fats and oils consist of straight chains of carbon atoms with all the leftover hooks linked to hydrogen atoms. If you're wondering what 'saturated' means with regard to fat, it's when all the carbon atoms are linked by single bonds so all the hooks are used up. Unsaturated means that there are some double bonds that can open up and react with something else.

In sugars the carbon atoms hold hands in a ring with a few oxygen atoms thrown in. There are less leftover hooks in this arrangement so there aren't as many hydrogen atoms needed to mop them up. Starch is a mixture of substances in which the rings in sugars have linked together to form large lumpy molecules. Sugars and starch are lumped together by nutritionists and called 'carbohydrate'.

Burn Baby, Burn

We get energy by burning the hydrogen and carbon in big carbohydrate molecules with the oxygen in the air. This makes water (water is one atom of oxygen connected to two atoms of hydrogen – you could call it oxygen hydride or di-hydrogen monoxide but nobody does) and carbon dioxide (which is one carbon atom with two oxygen molecules tacked on to it). Of course, there's no little pilot light burning in our insides and the hydrogen isn't in the form of a gas. What's happening is a very complicated process called digestion. There are two distinct parts to digestion: the physical and the biochemical.

Physical digestion is the bit we're most familiar with. It starts by us chomping up the food between our teeth; we then swallow it where it goes into the stomach to sit for a while; it's then ejected from the stomach out into the bowel where eventually what's left comes out the other end.

The biochemistry is happening at the same time. In the mouth the saliva isn't just a lubricant, it also starts the chemical reactions that separate the food into its constituent molecules. In the stomach the attack really gets going and the molecules are broken down until they're small enough to pass through the semi-permeable membrane (remember them from the bit about osmosis and salt?) that makes up the walls of the stomach and small intestine. As the food molecules pass through the walls of the stomach and intestines they are taken up into the bloodstream.

Our bodies run on glucose, which is a type of sugar. The liver is the place where all the big, rambling sugar and starch molecules are broken down into glucose units. The glucose can then travel round in the blood to wherever it's needed. When it gets there it's put on a conveyor belt of reactions that slowly chip away at it until there's nothing left but water and carbon dioxide. This is all done by fancy little chemicals, called enzymes, that keep tight control over what's happening at all stages. It's the equivalent of burning fuel in an engine to get power. Nature has found a way of getting the same effect without resorting to the high temperatures and pressures that you get in an engine so that we don't need to be made of steel and weigh a ton.

Enzymes work by being a precise shape that holds onto a molecule and presents it to other molecules in such a way that the reactions work at the low temperatures and pressures that we find inside us. This means that each step on the conveyor belt for burning glucose has a different enzyme. In fact, every chemical reaction in our bodies has several unique enzymes to make it work – there are a lot of enzymes in there. By the way, this burning is called oxidation because the end result is the addition of oxygen.

This conveyor belt happens to be circular. Some of the intermediate chemicals get used again and keep going round in a loop. Other chemicals pop into the loop at various points and the energy carrying molecules and the waste products (water and carbon dioxide) get spat out at various other points. The process is named the Krebs cycle, after Sir Hans Krebs who discovered it. The important thing, as far as we're concerned, is that the Krebs cycle only works properly on glucose. This means that the liver has to turn starch into its constituent sugars and any sugars that aren't glucose have to be turned into glucose. This is why it's good to drink drinks that have a lot of glucose when you're ill, the glucose goes straight into the energy system with hardly any digestion.

So, as far as energy is concerned, we can live on sugar and starch alone, but we don't. We also eat fat. Paradoxically, although fat can give about twice as much energy as the equivalent weight of carbohydrate, we don't digest it very well. Each fat molecule is chipped away, two carbon atoms at a time, until the molecules are small enough to tap into the

Krebs cycle. However, these molecules don't fit in the cycle at the same place as glucose and the cycle isn't closed properly. We need a large proportion of carbohydrate to keep the cycle going and then the fat molecules can be passed through the system without any problems. If there's no carbohydrate the Krebs cycle stops and the fat causes a build up of poisonous breakdown products.

Eating a large proportion of fat is a bad thing for two reasons. First, as we have just seen, our digestive systems are not very well equipped to deal with it and, second, it's too easy. If we eat a lot of fat we can easily take in more fuel than we need to keep warm, move about and repair ourselves. Because fat is such a compact source of energy nature uses it to store food until it's needed and this is the fat that we see on our bottoms and waists. The liver can convert fat to carbohydrate and carbohydrate to fat so you can still get overweight if you eat more carbohydrate than you need.

Keep Off The Grass
Why can't we eat grass and leaves and wood when we're surrounded by them? Plants get their strength from cellulose and similar chemicals such as lignin. These are stiff and make good strong structures and chemically they are very similar to starch and are really carbohydrates. The difference is in the shape and arrangement of the molecules.

Cellulose is really up tight. In cellulose all the molecules are straight and they sit in bundles with other molecules to make straight fibres. Starch, on the other hand, is like, laid back, man. In starch the molecules branch off every which way and sit around in a tangled heap. The result of this is that cellulose is very resistant to chemical attack so we can't get any energy from it. On the other hand starch breaks down fairly easily and it's our major source of energy.

The only way we can eat cellulose is to find some way to break it down first and the best way to do that is to pass it through a cow. Cows have complex digestive systems that can break down cellulose and we can eat cows and their milk. In fact, to be boringly accurate, even cows can't digest cellulose. What happens is that cows have bacteria in their stomachs that can digest cellulose and the cows digest the bacteria. This is why cows and elephants are big because they need a large amount of grass fermenting away inside them to get the energy they need.

This is my argument against vegetarianism. Eating meat and dairy products is our way of processing the biggest source of food on the planet, namely grass. (Of course, if the animals we eat are fed on grain and kept in abominable conditions then eating meat isn't such a good thing.) But to make things complicated it turns out that we do need to take in some cellulose directly. It's called dietary fibre and it seems to help with the physical side of digestion by giving the large intestine something to work on. You get dietary fibre from wholemeal bread, whole cereals, bran and some fruits and vegetables. You may come across the phrase 'available carbohydrate' which means the carbohydrate we can digest like sugar and starch; fibre is the opposite of this and is 'unavailable carbohydrate'.

Body Building

So far I've only looked at food as a source of energy. We also use it to repair our bodies, to grow and to make babies, all of which are similar occupations. Plants are mostly made of cellulose which gives them all the shape and structure they need while we, like all animals, are made of muscle, bone, cartilage, fat, and various complicated squidgy bits. The molecules that make all this possible are the proteins. Proteins are very complicated and there are lots of them. I've already mentioned one important set of proteins, and that's the enzymes. Muscles, tendons, cartilage and organs are made of protein while bones are built up by the action of proteins on inorganic chemicals. The trick with proteins is that each one has a unique and precise shape which enables it to interact in a controlled way with other proteins and other substances.

Nature makes proteins by a technique very like a computer program. All the information about the chemical composition of each protein and when to make it and under what circumstances is coded in another chemical called DNA (Deoxyribonucleic acid if you want to impress your chums). This is the material that we pass on, as genes, to our children and it's what makes them into copies of us. DNA doesn't list every atom and its location for each protein. Instead the proteins are built from about twenty different modules called amino acids and the DNA decides which of these to use to make each protein.

As far as food is concerned we need to know two things about proteins. One is that, although we can make any protein out of its constituent amino acids, we can only make about half the amino acids from scratch; we have to eat the rest ready made (nutritionists call them 'essential' amino acids). The other thing about proteins is that they have nitrogen in them. We break down proteins just as we break down carbohydrate and fat but we don't just get water and carbon dioxide we also get ammonia which is one nitrogen atom hooked up to three hydrogen atoms. This is seriously poisonous so we have to make it safe and get rid of it by turning it into urea, a relatively harmless chemical, which we then piddle out with our excess water.

Some proteins, especially enzymes, use elements other than carbon, hydrogen, oxygen and nitrogen to get the shapes that they need. These elements are usually metals and include iron, zinc, copper, manganese and magnesium, although we also need some non metallic elements such as iodine and fluorine. These elements have to be provided in tiny amounts in our food and they are called minerals when the quantity is relatively high, like iron or zinc, and trace elements when the quantity is really small.

There are some other chemicals that we can't make for ourselves and these are called vitamins. Vitamins are a rag bag of organic chemicals that have been found to be necessary for health for various reasons. They have been given letters which don't make much sense because of the history of their discovery.

At first they found two types of vitamins. One lot were found dissolved in fat and they were called 'A', the other lot were dissolved in water and they were called 'B'. This covers everything because if it doesn't dissolve in fat or water we can't digest it. Later they found that each of these categories actually held several chemicals so they made more categories. The 'B' vitamin group was broken down into a bunch of chemicals and each chemical was given a name or a number, or both. Vitamin 'C' was tacked on because although it is water soluble it didn't fit in with the 'B' group. Vitamins 'D','E' and 'K' are fat soluble but different from 'A'. I've laid them all out in a table with their chemical names. These names are of absolutely no use to you as a cook but they are interesting if you want to decipher the side of a cornflakes packet.

The Vitamins				
Letter	Name	Soluble in	What happens if it's not there?	Name of Disease caused by its deficiency
'A'	Retinol	Fat	Poor night vision, blindness, bad skin	
'B' B_1	Thiamin	Water	Can't digest carbohydrate	BeriBeri
B_2	Riboflavin		Can't release energy from food	
	Niacin		Can't release energy from food	Pellagra
B_6	Pyridoxine		Can't make proteins	
B_{12}			Can't make blood and nerve cells	Pernicious Anaemia
	Folic Acid		Can't make blood cells	Megaloblastic Anaemia
	Pantothenic Acid		Can't release energy from food	
	Biotin		Can't digest fat	
'C'	Ascorbic Acid	Water	Breakdown of blood vessels	Scurvy
'D' D_2	Ergocalciferol	Fat	Weak bones	Rickets
D_3	Cholecalciferol			
'E'	Alpha-tocopherol	Fat	Not a lot	
'K'		Fat	Blood won't clot	

Extra folic acid should be taken by women who expect to conceive as it protects against the baby developing spina bifida and other similar defects of the central nervous system.

Water, Water Everywhere

If you've started to look at the labels on packaged food you'll have noticed that where the nutrition information gives the weight of carbohydrate, fat, protein and fibre per hundred grams it often doesn't add up to a hundred grams and can be a lot less. I've told you about all the components of food, so what's left? It's water. We are well over half water ourselves so it's no surprise that our food also has some water in it. We need to turn over a lot of water every day to keep healthy. We keep the concentration of water in our bodies constant by controlling the input to compensate for the losses.

Most of the input comes from drinking water but there is a bit from the water content of food and even less from the chemical reactions from breaking down food. The losses are from sweating, from the moisture in our breath and from urinating. Sweat keeps you cool by evaporating off your skin. It needs heat to do this (latent heat again) and it gets the heat from your skin which cools down. The fine control of your water content is from the concentration and quantity of your urine. You have to pass some water to get rid of the breakdown products from digesting proteins.

I find that I'm most comfortable if I drink a lot and pee a lot. I believe many headaches and stomach disorders are caused by too little water. It has to be water. Alcohol makes you pee more than you drink (it's a 'diuretic') so you get dehydrated if you drink a lot of it. Tea, coffee and cola are also diuretics, to a lesser extent. Soft drinks and even natural fruit juices have a lot of sugar in them and we've already decided that too much sugar is bad for you. Sugar free drinks have a lot of artificial sweeteners and I'm a bit suspicious of those as well so you can't win.

How To Eat

After reading that bit on nutrition you might be thinking: 'How can I possibly keep track of that lot?' Fortunately you don't have to. Most of us eat what is called a 'balanced diet' in which we have a mixture of different foods and this automatically gives us everything we need. It's only people with special needs or restricted diets that need to know what extras they might be missing. Typical examples of people with special needs are pregnant women and growing children who may need extra calcium and protein. Some people choose to restrict their diets for religious or moral reasons. Strict vegans, who eat no meat or animal or fish products, have to watch out that they have all their essential amino acids because some are only naturally available in animal products. Some people, such as diabetics, have to restrict their diet for medical reasons and they also need to understand the details of nutrition.

Now a quick run down on what you ought to be eating:

1. The bulk of your food should be carbohydrate. You get this from cereals such as wheat and rice and starchy vegetables such as potatoes. Bread is a good source of carbohydrate but cakes and biscuits are not because they also have lots of fat and sugar. Sugar is a source of carbohydrate but it's too easy to eat too much and it doesn't have any fibre or vitamins. It also rots your teeth.
2. Eat some food with fat in it but try to keep the amount down. Cheese, butter, margarine and cream are almost entirely fat. Meat and nuts are very high in fat and just about all snacks and nice things have a high fat content. In fact, most processed foods have a lot of fat in them. If you don't know what is in a packet of processed food look at the label on the side, it will show the relative amounts of carbohydrate, fat, protein and fibre. Look at the listing that says 'grams per 100 grams of product', anything over about 15 grams is high fat.
3. We need some protein in our diet because we can't make all the protein building blocks in our own bodies. We get most of our protein from meat, fish and dairy products but we can also get some from whole wheat, brown rice, nuts, and beans. Vegans have to be careful to get enough of the right kinds of proteins that have the 'essential amino acids'. The normal western diet has much more protein than we need so if we cut down on meat and dairy products to reduce our fat intake the reduction of protein won't do any harm.
4. Although we don't get any energy or building blocks from it we need some fibre for the physical part of our digestion. Fibre is found in whole wheat and brown rice and in most fruit and vegetables.
5. The only other thing to know about is minerals and vitamins. One reason that we need to eat some fatty foods is because that is the only way to get the fat soluble vitamins. You'll find them in dairy products, meat (especially offal)

and oily fish like herring and mackerel. Of the water soluble vitamins the 'B' series are found in just about everything and you need to be on a particularly junky diet not to get enough. Vitamin 'C' is mostly found in citrus fruit and it has been suggested that mammoth doses can do us good. The water soluble vitamins are easily lost in cooking so you should eat some raw fruit and be careful when cooking vegetables. It has been suggested that modern, western methods of farming are raising vegetables that do not have enough minerals, especially zinc. You shouldn't need to go out of your way for vitamins or minerals but if you're worried about them take capsules of multivitamins and minerals.

How To Lose Weight

I couldn't write a book about food without a bit about losing weight, the great obsession of the western world. The first thing you should know is that

LOSING WEIGHT IS NOT EASY.

Be very sceptical of any scheme or method that promises instant, easy weight loss.

Our bodies are finely tuned to keep a constant weight. The energy input in the form of food has to exactly match the output in the form of muscle action, heat and repair of our bodies. Our bodies have complex control systems to keep the input and output balanced. They work on a principle called 'homeostasis' by doctors and 'negative feedback' by engineers. The idea is that there's a value for your weight stored away somewhere and, if you exceed that value, mechanisms are triggered either to stop you eating so much or to use up more fuel, or both. In some people this works perfectly and they stay just the weight they want to be all their lives; in most people it's a disaster.

Two things can happen to make you over or under weight. One: your internal weight could be set wrong. Two: you could be ignoring the signals and eating the wrong amounts or doing the wrong amount of exercise. If it's the second reason it should be fairly easy to settle into the right weight because you'll be working with your body. If it's the first reason you've got problems because you'll have a constant battle to keep your weight away from its set point. This is what happens to most of us. Nobody knows if it's possible to change your internal weight value or if it stays constant through your life. It's best to assume the worst, that the set point doesn't just stay the same, it actually increases as we get older. This explains why we get fat as we get older, even though we eat about the same amount.

In spite of this it is possible to lose weight. The basis of losing weight is to make the input less than the output and the first step is to cut down the amount of high energy food that we eat. This isn't enough on its own because those highly tuned mechanisms will do everything they can to keep your weight constant. The main thing that happens is that you'll tend to avoid using your muscles and move around less, maybe even sleep. You might also feel cold. This is because we are hot blooded creatures and our bodies are kept at a higher temperature than our surroundings (unless our surroundings are very hot). We generate the heat from our muscles when we're active but when we're motionless some special stuff called brown fat keeps us warm. This brown fat goes through all the motions of using up fuel, like a muscle, but doesn't produce any movement, only heat. The action of the brown fat tends to fine tune our heat output and it has been suggested that obese people haven't any brown fat, or what they have doesn't work.

This leads to the recipe for weight loss (this is the only recipe in the book). It needs to be a two pronged attack: cut down the input by eating less high energy food, especially fat, and increase the output by doing more exercise. You have to do both these things, just one won't do the trick. It's not all bad news. Surprisingly, exercise doesn't make you hungry and the increase in muscle tone will make you look slimmer and feel better even if your weight doesn't change much. The other good news is that you can eat large quantities of carbohydrates (but you must cut out nearly all the fat and go easy on the sugar). The knowledge of food and cooking you've gained from this book should enable you to make good meals with a low fat content but it's very difficult if you only eat processed food.

You have to keep up this lifestyle of high exercise and low fat otherwise your body weight will drift back to its original value and will probably increase as you get older. I know this works because I've done it – but I also know how easy it is to drift back 'cos I've done that too!

8

IN THE BEST POSSIBLE TASTE

Variety Is The Spice Of Life

I've saved the most interesting and exciting bit till last. Flavour is what turns food from fuel into fun. The cruellest punishment you can give someone is to condemn them to live on bread and water (and I don't mean lovely, crusty, wholemeal bread). Most of us need variety and want each meal to taste different, although, judging by the success of various burger bars, a lot of us do like our food to be identical every time.

So far we've covered the technology of cooking, getting the structure and nutrition right. However, the real art and skill of cooking is in controlling the flavour. All food has flavour but it's usually not enough. We soon get bored with the unadorned flavour of simple foods and want more excitement. This is why we add ingredients that do nothing for the food other than change its flavour. These ingredients usually have such strong, concentrated flavours that we wouldn't dream of eating them on their own (in fact, some are downright nasty).

Taste And Aroma

Flavour is a combination of taste and aroma. Taste is the sensation that we get directly from the sensors in our mouths, called taste buds, and aroma is a fancy word for smell. The range of tastes is very limited – they are: sweet, salt, sour and bitter – but the range of aromas is enormous. The combinations of taste, aroma, and other sensations such as texture (smooth, crunchy, chewy, etc.), heat (chemical or physical) or cold give an almost infinite variety of flavours. We have different sensitivities to the four tastes at different locations on our tongues and mouths. This means that the flavour of food can be changed by how we put it in our mouths. If you eat something like pizza first with a knife and fork then by picking up a big piece in your hands you'll see what I mean.

A similar thing happens with aroma. You smell the food through your nose as it approaches your lips but you also smell it through the back of your nose from inside your mouth which gives a different sensation. You'll notice this effect if you drink from a can or bottle instead of from a glass, the flavours are subtly different. The Belgians have made a big deal out of this. They are nuts on beer and they have a beer for every occasion and circumstance. There are thousands! Each beer has its own glass and each glass is a different shape. Some recent research has discovered that the shape of the glass can enhance or diminish the flavour of the beer. Most of the older breweries got it right and chose a design of glass that presented their beer in the best way. Unfortunately, some of the younger ones (that is, less than two hundred years old), in their efforts to be different, chose the wrong shape of glass.

Texture is also more important than we realise. Think of the difference between a sugar cube and candy floss. They are both made of sugar but they hit the mouth in completely different ways. The sugar cube is hard, crunchy and spiky while candy floss is soft, and yielding. Another example is the difference between Cheddar cheese at room temperature compared to when it has been cooked. Two things are happening here: at room temperature the texture of the cheese is dominated by the hard fat that it's made of; at higher temperatures the fat melts into a liquid oil but the proteins coagulate and form a new solid structure with a different texture. Of course, the coagulation of the protein also changes its flavour but that only goes to show how complicated this business is.

Getting Personal
Taste alone, without considering aroma, gives us some basic but important information about our food. The ability to detect sweet food leads us towards the high energy carbohydrates while bitterness is usually associated with poisons. We often spit out bitter food, without even thinking about it, but we never spit out sweet food. The sour taste comes from acids. Acids are the stereotype deadly, dangerous, corrosive chemical but, in real life, it's only the strong mineral acids like nitric and sulphuric

that are dangerous. Acids are just chemicals and there are weak ones as well as strong. The most common in food are acetic acid (the main component of vinegar) and citric acid (which is found in fruit). In nature, sourness is usually associated with unripe fruit so it's worth leaving it alone until it tastes sweet. The salt detector is there simply because we need some salt in our diet.

Taste only works on substances that are dissolved in water. If they aren't already dissolved we provide the water in the form of saliva. We detect the presence of fat by its texture in the mouth (the Japanese call this sensation 'Umami'). We can't taste it because it doesn't dissolve in water. Starch doesn't taste of anything which is why it's boring to eat on its own and we always add something tasty to it. Nature makes sure we eat starch by its effect on our stomach – it's the most effective food for making us feel full so that we don't need to eat any more.

All this gives a few hints on what we like to eat and why. We like sweet food because it gives us energy and we like the texture of fats for the same reason. We like salt and we don't like sour and bitter tastes. This makes perfect evolutionary and biological sense. The difficult bit is why do we eat sour, bitter and hot foods? The only hypothesis I can come up with is that we are obligate omnivores. This is a fancy way of saying that, not only are we able to eat anything, but that we HAVE to try and eat everything we come across. The biological reason for this is probably that we need essential amino acids, vitamins and minerals that don't come from any one source – we can only get all we need by eating everything we can get. This seeking for variety isn't necessary for our day to day existence any more, as most of us get a balanced diet with all the nutrients we need but the desire is still there.

Just as we are all different shapes and sizes we also have different sensitivities to taste and smell. This can be seen as differences in overall sensitivity and also as an exceptional sensitivity or a complete lack of sensitivity to one or more individual tastes or smells. In fact, it has been suggested that each one of us is unable to detect at least one of the many individual smells. The medical people call this 'anosmia' (which I think is a brilliant word) but I tend to think of it as 'smell blindness', as a parallel to colour blindness. This means that what you taste may not be the same as what other people taste. There's not much you can do about this, just remember it can happen and be sympathetic if someone doesn't like what you've cooked.

Taste is a crude tool. It can only distinguish four chemical types. Aroma, on the other hand, has almost infinite discrimination. We can detect thousands of chemicals by their smell at very low concentrations and when mixed with other smelly chemicals, although compared with other animals, such as dogs, our sense of smell is pretty feeble. Aroma allows us to pin down, much more exactly, what it is we are eating. This goes back to us being omnivores. We have to be able to tell what is good to eat from what is bad and, given a choice, we have to pick the best. Taste can only give us a broad brush indication of what's good and what's bad. Using our other senses – smell, vision and touch for texture – we can identify all kinds of substances, including potential foods. Hearing isn't much use for this, unless we're detecting rice krispies. Hearing's much more useful for preventing us from being eaten by something else!

Rats are similar to us in that they are omnivores. Rats will take a small sample of any new substance they come across and, if it doesn't make them sick, they'll eat more until it becomes an important part of their diet. Some substances are edible but not immediately poisonous so the rat will wait a while to see if there's a delayed effect. If something does make a rat sick he'll avoid it and never try it again. We are the same as rats in that, when faced with a new food candidate, we'll try a little bit and see what happens. If we're sick later on we'll never touch that food again. This can be a mistake. Some people will never touch fish, for example, because they once had a bout of food poisoning after a fish meal. There's no guarantee that the fish caused the sickness, or that eating fish will cause it again, but this mechanism is so strong that it won't respond to logic. (Strangely enough this doesn't work with alcohol. People who drink a lot are often made very sick by alcohol and they know, damn well, what caused it but it doesn't put them off. They may say 'Never again' but they don't mean it.)

The point of all this rigamarole is that this technique of trying food and gradually adding it to our repertoire of suitable scoff only works if we can discriminate and recall quite small differences in flavour. Since it's a matter of survival, evolution has trained our sense of taste and smell to a high pitch of sensitivity. We get pleasure from stretching our ability to use all our senses:

we like to look at pictures and scenery, we like to listen to music, we like to feel textures and we like to try new flavours.

A Flavour Spectrum

I said, right at the beginning of this book, that I like to categorise things. I also like to put things in order and I've always felt that there must be some way of putting flavours in order to make something like a rainbow or a colour wheel. Well, I've tried very hard and it's not easy. The main problem is that most of the flavours we are familiar with are really combinations of tastes and aromas and it's difficult to tease them apart. Take fruit, for example. The flavour of fruit is mostly a mixture of sugar and citric acid and a simple mixture of those two chemicals gives a pretty good imitation of a lemon. But what's the difference between a lemon and an orange? It actually comes down to a quite subtle aroma which wouldn't be out of place as a spice. In fact, expert chefs use the thin, coloured layer of skin off the outside of oranges and lemons (called the zest) as a sweet spice.

I decided, after much agonizing, that there aren't really all that many significantly different aromas. There are just a few groups and within each group there is a gradation of strength. It gets complicated because natural products may have combinations of more than one aroma and that may be superimposed on one or more tastes. This means that these natural products can't always be put into a single group; some of them overlap several groups.

These are my groups. You don't have to agree with them, but here they are anyway with some examples:

Aromas		
Oniony	Onion, Garlic, Spring Onion, Shallot, Chive, Leek	
Herby	Oregano, Basil, Tarragon, Rosemary, Thyme, Parsley, Sage, Mint	
Spicy	Sweet	Ginger, Nutmeg, Cinnamon, Mace, Vanilla
	Curry	Saffron, Coriander, Cumin, Caraway
	Aromatic	Aniseed, Liquorice, Coffee, Chocolate

Flowery	Lavender, Rose, Violet, Orange, Lemon	
Meaty	Red Meat	Beef, Venison, Lamb, Bear
	White Meat	Pork, Chicken, Turkey, Snake
	White Fish	Cod, Haddock, Sole
	Oily Fish	Herring, Mackerel
Dairy	Milk, Cream, Cheese, Egg, Butter	
Nutty	Nuts, Seeds, Bread, Cereals, Beer	
Foul	Strong Cheese, Durian, the little black bits from between your toes (not used in cooking)	

Tastes and Mouth Sensations	
Salt	Salt, Soy Sauce, Monosodium Glutamate
Sweet	Sugar, Fruit
Sour	Acid, Vinegar, Fruit
Bitter	Chicory, Hops, Lettuce, Coffee, Cocoa
Hot	Chilli, Pepper, Mustard, Horseradish, Ginger
Fat	Animal Fat, Meat, Vegetable Oil, Cream, Butter, Margarine

The point about these groups is not that they are definitive or exhaustive but they can give you ideas of how to control the final flavour of your dish. If you're trying to reproduce a particular dish then you must stick to the recipe and use exactly the ingredients it says. If, on the other hand, you're just trying to cook, you can use what you like or, more likely, whatever's in the cupboard. This is where it gets creative.

Getting Creative
When you create a dish you're aiming for a balance of flavour somewhere between bland and overpowering. There's quite a lot of room for manoeuvre in there but it does depend on your audience. People who are used to curries and chilli will demand hot food but their friends, who have never tried

anything stronger than custard, will find even the mildest
curry overpowering.

Don't assume that you have to add flavour. Most food has a
flavour of its own that's easily swamped by strong flavoured
ingredients. Try your fish, meat or vegetables cooked simply,
without any added flavour, and see what you think. If it's too
bland start with the simplest flavours first. Try a little salt, the
classic flavour enhancer, it might be all you need. This doesn't
mean that you should put salt on everything. Try it first.

Salt is like fat and sugar in that our natural desire to eat as
much of them as possible is causing us trouble. In the wild,
where humans used to live tens of thousands of years ago, salt,
sugar and fat were rare so we would eat all we could find. Now
they are common and we still eat all we can find and we end up
eating too much. I've already explained how too much fat and
sugar makes us fat. Too much salt, on the other hand, is believed
to be linked with high blood pressure and heart disease in some
people. The thing is, we don't need all that much salt. There's no
danger of not getting enough in the typical western diet, so it's
worth cutting down. I cut down on my salt intake several years
ago and an interesting thing happened. At first everything tasted
really bland, as you'd expect, but quite soon, after a few days, I
got used to it and found that I could taste subtleties of flavour
that I hadn't noticed before. I would recommend to anyone that
they cut down on salt – don't add it to any dish unless it's really
horrible without and don't add any at the table until you've tried
the food and decided that you really want it. The only problem is
that snacks such as crisps and nuts taste far too salty to me now.

Salt is an example of an ingredient that enhances the flavour
of the food that it's mixed with. Many of the spices have a
similar effect. In fact, if you can taste the spice you've probably
put too much in. What you're aiming for is to increase the
intensity of the flavour of the underlying food without swamp-
ing it with the flavour ingredients. It's another balancing act.
The only way to get the knack is to try it and, as I've already
said, if you get it the way you like it, it might not suit your dinner
guests. In that case you might have to compromise by cutting
back the quantities of your favourite ingredients. One thing you
can do is to put the strong flavoured ingredients out separately,
as a sort of relish, then everyone can have as much, or as little, as
they want. As well as salt the flavour enhancing ingredients

include pepper, mustard and monosodium glutamate (usually in the form of Soy sauce). These ingredients are often found on the table to be added to suit personal taste.

A thing that I've found helpful is to taste the flavour ingredients, undiluted, to get a sense of just how strong they are and what flavour they are adding to the dish. Some of these, particularly the hot ones, are so strong that it's difficult to reconcile the raw taste with what you'll get in the resulting dish but I think the experience helps you to balance out the flavours. Don't forget to sniff as well; the aroma of these ingredients is what makes them special and you should make yourself familiar with the smells. Be careful with the hot ones such as chilli and pepper or you could hurt your hooter.

Compare And Contrast

All through this book I've tried to guide and suggest rather than instruct and I'm not going to stop now. Only you can decide the flavours that you like in your food but I can tell you what works and what usually doesn't. We'll start with some basics.

Foods such as potato, bread, rice and pasta, which are mainly starchy carbohydrate, are very bland and need a little salt. I once forgot the salt when I made some bread and it was quite nasty (I haven't done that again). Fatty food gets combined with just about anything to make it more palatable. Cheese is mainly fat with a large dose of salt which makes it easier to eat than cream or lard, for example. Acids, such as vinegar or lemon juice, are put on fatty foods to 'cut' the fatty taste; think of the vinegar which helps the fish and chips go down. Salad dressings, such as vinaigrette or mayonnaise, are oil combined with the acid vinegar. Sugar combines well with fat, as we have seen in the section on baking, but the combination is also found in sweets like toffee and chocolate.

Sugar on its own is pretty overwhelming and we've developed all sorts of ways to make sugar more palatable. One obvious way is to combine it with its opposites in taste. Sweet and salt is not common, although it's found in some Norwegian confectionery and in Chinese preserved fruit; it's an acquired taste! Sweet and sour is often used, especially in Chinese style cooking. Sweet and bitter is so common that we don't notice it: many of us put sugar into tea or coffee to counteract the bitterness (or is drinking tea and coffee an excuse for eating more sugar?) and don't forget that chocolate is quite bitter – taste some cocoa powder if you don't believe me.

Beware of these food combinations if you are trying to keep slim because they all make high energy foods easier to eat so we eat more of them. Imagine how many chocolate biscuits you'd eat if you had to eat the cocoa powder, flour, margarine and sugar separately.

Once you've got the basics sorted out you'll want to experiment with herbs and spices and stuff. If you get the balance of flavours right it doesn't matter what you chuck in, it will work, but there are some things you can learn from tradition. It's usually best to put in a selection of similar herbs or spices rather than a lot of just one. For example, don't just use oregano; put in some basil and maybe parsley or rosemary as well. If you're doing a curry put in a selection of curry spices such as cumin, coriander and fenugreek. It's better to make up your own mixtures instead of buying a ready made mix for two reasons. First, it's not very creative using someone else's selection of flavours, it doesn't leave you any control; and second, many of the mixtures are not very good and don't keep well.

Garlic goes well in anything and the smell announces to the whole world that there's some serious cooking going on. There's a strange fear of garlic among some English people that I have trouble understanding. I think it's something to do with not wanting to smell like a Frenchman. Be that as it may, there are some people (and they're not necessarily vampires) who will be put off by the slightest whiff of garlic and may well not set foot in your house. It's up to you how you deal with this but, be warned, it does happen. Everybody else loves garlic and it's an important part of just about every cuisine in the world (except English). As with the other herbs and spices, garlic goes well with other oniony flavours especially onion itself. Garlic also combines well with hot spices such as chilli and ginger.

As well as combining similar flavours you can deliberately contrast them. We've already discussed sweet and sour, sweet and bitter, salt and bland, where the mixture averages out in intensity. The alternative is to keep the contrasting flavours separate so that you have different taste sensations in different parts of your mouth. The sort of thing where this works is to have pieces of fruit in a savoury dish or to have whole peppercorns or pieces of sea salt scattered about.

It's possible to have too much variety of flavours, then you get what I call the brown plasticine effect. You must remember playing with plasticine as a child, and you'll have noticed that, no matter what colours you start with, once you've mixed a few pieces together, it always comes out brown, and not a very nice brown at that. The same thing can happen with flavours. If you mix a lot of them together you end up with an overall flavour with no individual character at all and which doesn't taste of anything in particular. I've noticed this with many processed foods and, oddly enough, it's often worse in the upmarket ones which have a lot of fancy ingredients.

There's a positive side to the brown plasticine effect where you get a new flavour which doesn't seem to be related to the flavour of any of the ingredients. This can be a wonderful thing but obviously it's very difficult to predict. The best you can do is to try and remember what you put in and see if you can do it again. Some quite surprising combinations work very well together and you might already know of some of them. Ones I've come across include: beer and olives, peanut butter and jam, peanut butter and bananas, Guinness and condensed milk, cheese and pineapple, chicken and cocoa. Try anything – you've got as much chance of creating a classic as anybody.

Getting Fresh
Using herbs means using the leaves and sometimes the stems and flowers of various plants. The flavours are in the oils that are found there. Like all leaves, herbs don't keep once they've been plucked from the plant they're growing on. They'll last a few days in the fridge but they lose the flavour oils very quickly. The herbs you buy in little glass jars in the shops are dried and don't have the same flavour.

I have a problem with laziness here. Ideally you should grow your own herbs and pick them from your garden or window box when you need them. I'm not very good at growing plants so I don't do that and I also can't be bothered with trying to use fresh herbs from the shops when I have dried ones in my cupboard. So, although I've just been preaching to you about how important fresh herbs are, I don't use them. I suggest you try it for yourself. If you think the difference is worth the effort then carry on. But if you think dried herbs are good enough then don't be bullied into faffing about with fresh ones.

Spices are dried bits of various plants. Most of them are seeds or berries but some are roots or other bits. Spices last much better than herbs but they still lose their flavour over time. Ideally you should grind the spices as you need them. Again, I'm lazy but I do use fresh ground pepper and I've noticed that the ground spices that you get in those ubiquitous little glass jars don't have much flavour.

One spice that I do make a fuss about is coffee. I like strong, intense flavours and that's how I like my coffee. I drink it without milk or sugar so I'm very sensitive to its quality. I've found that it doesn't matter how you make your coffee, in a jug, in a filter, in a cafetière or in an espresso machine, what matters is the freshness of the beans.

As soon as the beans are roasted they start to deteriorate by losing the volatile flavour oils and by air reacting with what's left. Grinding the beans makes this happen much faster. I've found that the only way to get the coffee I like is to roast the beans myself in small quantities (about 50 grams or 2 ounces at a time). I keep the roasted beans in the freezer in a plastic bag with the air squeezed out and I grind the beans just before I use them. I only go to these lengths because I've personally tested each step and found that I can tell the difference and I prefer the hard way. You might find it's all a waste of time and stick with instant.

Hot, Hot, Hot

Hot spices deserve a special mention. I'm mystified as to why we like hot food but I've no doubt that we do. It seems to be addictive in that you get used to it and then you need a bigger dose to get the effect until you don't want to eat anything that isn't hot. All cultures have their hot food and if they don't they hijack the cuisine of a culture that does. Traditional English cooking must be the least spicy of all cuisines but English mustard is far stronger than any other and the English embraced Indian curries as soon as they came across them. It's the same in America. The white settlers were originally from northern Europe but when they mixed with the Spanish influenced Mexicans in Texas they fell in love with chilli.

I believe that the heat isn't so much a flavour as a mouth sensation and it can be quite painful. The sensation is felt in different places depending on the spice causing it. I've found that chilli affects the front of my mouth and my lips; mustard and horseradish go straight to the back of my nose; pepper seems to go to the front of my nose; ginger works on the back of my throat. This means that a mixture of these spices will give a general burn all over your mouth, nose and throat. In sufficient quantity any of them make your eyes water and chilli is notorious for passing all the way through your body and still burning on the way out.

Once you're used to the heat the benefit is that there are flavours you can't get any other way and, speaking as a kebab addict, they're pretty wonderful. Hot spices don't have much flavour of their own but they do enhance whatever they are mixed with. It may be that the damage caused to the taste buds makes them more sensitive. Unlike with salt, I haven't heard of any medical problems with hot spices and I would recommend anyone who likes food to build up a tolerance to them so that they can appreciate the flavours. If you cook your own food it's easy to put in the amount of chilli, or whatever, to suit your preference and gradually build it up until you can go to your local kebab shop or curry house and order with confidence.

9

AROUND THE WORLD

The Same Only Different
I thought, when I started on this book, that it would be easy to
categorise various cooking styles from different parts of the
world and pin down the essence of what makes Indian, Chinese,
Mexican, French, English, or any other country's, cooking
distinctive. But the more I looked into it the more I found how
difficult it was. Cooking styles don't stick to political boundaries any more than any other natural phenomenon does. What I
did find were some universal trends and influences that have
operated over the whole world. The interactions that these
trends and influences have with local plants and animals are
what makes each local cuisine different.

First something blindingly obvious: people only eat what they
can get. Nowadays anyone with enough money can get anything
from anywhere, so location isn't the absolute deciding factor it
used to be. What you find is that traditional food and cooking
styles reflect the limitations that people had in the past so, for
example, people that live by the sea eat a lot of fish. It can be very
difficult to unravel what is truly local from what has been introduced or imported from other regions because travellers and
colonists always tried to take their own local styles and ingredients
with them. In many cases the introduced food completely wipes
out the native one. It's hard to imagine what British cookery must
have been like without the potato but, of course, it was only
brought over from America in the 16th century. Similarly, chilli is
a native of Mexico but now it's found everywhere.

North And South
The first worldwide trend that I've noticed is that food gets more

spicy as you get nearer the equator. I don't know why this is. One reason may simply be that the strong flavoured plants are native to the tropics and grow more easily there or maybe the tropical climate means that food goes off more quickly so spices were used to cover up the rancid taste. Perhaps people needed something to perk up their appetites; if you live in a cold country you'll eat anything you can get and it doesn't need strong flavours to make you hungry. Anyway, there's a definite trend from the fiery curries of Indonesia and Malaysia, through the hot curries of southern India, to the more delicately flavoured cuisine of northern India, Iran and Turkey, ending in the relatively bland cooking of northern Europe. The trend can also be traced up the Pacific coast. The spiciness decreases as you move from Indonesia to Korea.

Northern countries tend to use pickles to add flavour and much needed vitamins through the winter. Before modern preserving techniques these pickles would have been essential for health and even for survival but now they are appreciated for their taste. You can see this in the similarity between the German Sauerkraut and the Korean Kimchee, both of which are basically pickled cabbage.

Another trend is that food gets more stodgy as you go away from the equator. Stodge is high energy food, usually some combination of fat and carbohydrate and it's just what you need to keep warm through a long cold winter. Typical stodge is steamed puddings, dumplings, pâtés and some kinds of sausage. There's nothing inherently wrong with stodge but it doesn't fit with our current lifestyle. Now that we live in centrally heated houses, work in air-conditioned offices and travel everywhere by car, we don't need much food for warmth so it's easy to eat too much if we eat stodge.

The traditional fats used in northern countries are from animals: beef, pork or dairy fats. Unfortunately these are saturated and it seems that they are implicated in causing heart disease. The fats people use in Mediterranean and tropical countries are more likely to be unsaturated, such as olive oil or groundnut oil, so they have less trouble with their hearts. In the far north the native Eskimo and Inuit didn't have heart problems until they changed from eating fish, which has mostly unsaturated fats, to eating the typical North American diet which is high in saturated animal fat. The Japanese have seen a similar trend. Even in a country as small as Britain there's a noticeable trend towards more stodge and saturated fat the further north you go.

In Aberdeen, in the north of Scotland, they've elevated the making of stodge to an art form. This is seen at its best in the chip shop. Like every chip shop in Britain the Aberdeen chippy sells chips and deep fried fish in batter, but they also have much more unhealthy things. The most common is the pudding which can be red, white, black or haggis. The black pudding is the same as black puddings found elsewhere, being mostly pig or sheep blood with pig fat and a binder such as oatmeal; white pudding is the same without the blood; while haggis has sheep offal such as heart and liver instead of blood. The red pudding is a fairly ordinary sausage and isn't so popular. In the chip shop these puddings are deep fried in batter so an already very fatty dish is made even fattier. Asking for a 'Haggis Supper' will get you a deep fried, battered haggis pudding with a helping of chips and, while it is wonderful, it shouldn't be eaten too often. Aberdonians will deep fry anything in batter, I've even heard that Mars bars cooked this way are popular and are eaten by school children for their lunches. Aberdeen also has a tradition of meat pies including the famous mutton pie which is the staple diet of many of the inhabitants. Aberdeen has the highest incidence of heart disease in Britain, if not the world.

East To West
As you go round the world, as opposed to up and down, you see the effects of history rather than climate. I reckon there are just a few basic styles of cooking and they are modified by the north-south effects and by the availability of local produce to give the multitude of different national cuisines that we see today. The basic styles are:

Persian: covers the area from Greece, through Turkey and Iran (where it originated) to Pakistan and northern India.

Mediterranean: found on the Mediterranean coasts of many countries including Spain, France, Italy, the Balkans, Greece, Turkey, Syria, Lebanon, Israel, Egypt, Libya, Tunisia, Algeria, Morocco and the islands (Majorca, Sicily, Corsica, Sardinia, Crete and Cyprus). This style also has an influence on South American and Southern USA cooking.

North European: starts in the south where the Mediterranean style leaves off and goes on up to the Arctic Circle taking in northern Italy, northern France, Britain, Belgium, Holland, Norway, Sweden, Denmark, Germany, Austria, Switzerland, Poland and Russia. The north European style has been transported to the northern states of the USA from where it has spread around the world.

Far East: covers Indonesia, Malaysia, Philippines, Vietnam, Cambodia, Thailand, Burma, China, Japan and Korea.

African: the whole of the African continent seems to have its own style.

There are no firm boundaries between these styles, they tend to blend together at the edges. The ease with which people can travel means that a style can even leap-frog over an area that has some other style and turn up thousands of miles away. People aren't purists about keeping to their own style of cooking. They do it because that's the way they were taught and because it usually suits the climate and the ingredients they can get locally. Although, as I've already said, you can get anything, anywhere, from anywhere, local produce is always cheaper and fresher.

Sometimes a new food ingredient will be introduced, either deliberately or accidentally, into a new area and, if it's better than the local food, it can completely take over. This happened with potatoes and with chillies which are now grown extensively around the world. When it happens it can be difficult to find out what food was there before and how it might have been cooked.

Where Do Kebabs Come From?

What I find surprising is the influence of Persian cuisine and the fact that we don't recognise that influence. Persia was, and still is, part of Iran and bears the same relationship to it as England does to Britain. Persia built up a strong empire which reached to northern India in the East and to Turkey in the West and they brought their style of eating with them. The influence of Persia reached further than that. They were great traders, best known for opening the 'Spice Road' all the way from the Pacific coast of China to the Atlantic coast of Europe. Obviously the main trading commodity was spices but along with the spices came information and some of that must have been about cooking. Until I learnt about the Persian influence I couldn't understand why Turkish Kebabs were almost identical to Indian ones although their origins were thousands of miles apart. Now I know – they're both out of Iran. You can see the influence in your local kebab shop, especially the Indian ones, from the names of things you find there: Nan is Persian for bread, Kebab means to grill and Tikka means a small piece. Even the word tandoori isn't Indian, it comes from Turkey where a tandir is a pit in the kitchen for cooking in. (The tandoori is a purpose built clay oven which is a refinement of the tandir.)

Persian food isn't hot in the spicy sense but it is fragrant and uses all the spices and herbs you can think of except the hot ones such as chilli, red pepper, ginger or garlic. For flavouring the Persians typically use spices including coriander seed, turmeric, cinnamon, cumin, cardamom and black pepper; herbs such as coriander, dill, mint, marjoram, tarragon, fenugreek, Persian chives, sweet basil and French parsley as well as various flowers (especially roses), orange peel and pistachio nuts.

The main bulk of a Persian meal is bread. With the bread they would have eaten stews or soups for flavour and – as we smugly know from our study of nutrition – essential protein, fat, vitamins and minerals. In fact bread is the main provider of carbohydrate for northern Indian and Turkish cooking as well. Rice is used but it's mostly for show and for fancy meals, it's not a main part of the diet. The Persians like large dumplings made of rice or Bulgar wheat and stuffed with surprises such as fruit and nuts.

In England, and it's probably the same almost everywhere, our impression of Indian and Turkish food is gained mostly from restaurants. We all know that restaurant cooking isn't the same as home cooking but we may not know what the differences are. The origins of restaurant cooking are in the palaces of the aristocracy where food was used to display wealth. This meant that the food had to be difficult to prepare, each dish had to be distinctively different from every other, unusual and expensive ingredients had to be used and everything had to look spectacular. Such showing off means that taste and wholesomeness can come second to gimmicks and we still see some of this in restaurants today.

This is why we associate Indian and Turkish food with rice although that isn't the way they eat at home. Rice is eaten as part of special celebration meals and would have been served more often in the palaces than in people's homes. Since restaurants come from this background instead of from home cooking we get a distorted view of what people would normally eat.

A restaurant will typically try to have the appearance of an overflowing banquet table by offering many apparently different dishes on the menu. Quite often these are only minor variations on a theme and can be put together from a selection of previously prepared ingredients to meet each order. The emphasis on meat also comes from the palace. Meat has always been expensive and the consumption of large amounts of it has always been seen as a sign of wealth. In a restaurant meal the meat becomes the focus while in a traditional home meal the bread is the most important food with meat being just another flavour ingredient.

Of course it's not only the Indians and Turks who have this tradition, it's also the basis of French 'Haute Cuisine' which has its roots in the powerful and rich French aristocracy. We see the same thing in French restaurants where food is prepared for effect and to impress rather than to feed. Don't get me wrong about this, I like restaurant food and I like the theatrical side of food presentation, but it's not the way real people cook every day. Going back to the main theme of this book, most cookery books are trying to show you how to cook to impress just like the chef in a palace or a fancy restaurant. Often this is trying to run before you can walk and can cause all sorts of grief in the kitchen.

As I've already said, Persian food isn't hot but then neither is all of Indian or Turkish food. The myth of the fiery Indian curry is an English creation. The people of Southern India like hot food but the ones who came to England and set up restaurants were mainly from the North of India and from Pakistan (which is on the north west border of India) and they eat in the Persian style. The story goes that the hot curry was the revenge of the restaurateurs on the drunken louts who came in for a curry after the pubs had shut. Being able to eat the hottest curry became a test of manhood (and an excuse to drink more lager) and soon the curries got ridiculously hot. There's nothing difficult in making a curry hot, you just add more chilli. If you're interested in the subtlety of Persian food try to find a good Indian restaurant and order something mild like Korma. In a good restaurant nothing will be painfully hot although a lot of the food will be quite spicy and the vegetable curries are often much hotter than meat ones. By the way, the word curry comes from the southern (Tamil speaking) part of India and is not part of the language of the people who set up the curry houses.

There's no mystery about curry, it's just a sauce. The distinctive smells and flavour come from a selection of spices, particularly cumin and fenugreek. Any curry sauce goes with any vegetables or any meat so feel free to experiment. Curry can be a bit overwhelming for fish so be careful and don't use a strong sauce. The curry spices can also be used in slow cooked stews to soften tough meat.

The other way that meat is typically eaten is grilled. The word kebab means to grill and is nothing to do with flaming spears or even small skewers. Cooking on a skewer is a convenient way to hold the meat over the fire and, provided metal skewers are used, they ensure that the middle of the meat is cooked. The kebab that you often see in England, with lumps of meat between lumps of vegetables, isn't traditional and was probably invented because it looks pretty. It doesn't work: the vegetables and the meat cook at different speeds and the meat juices don't mingle with the vegetables because the skewer is horizontal.

Genuine kebabs use chunks of meat threaded on the skewer (tikka is a typical example) or use mince pressed onto the skewer in a sausage shape, as in the seikh or shish kebab. For a tikka the meat is usually marinaded in a sauce which includes yoghurt and something acid, such as lemon juice, to tenderise the meat. The flavour comes from the usual herbs and spices which are also added to the mince to make shish kebabs.

The choice of meat is influenced by religion. The Moslems will not eat pork and the Hindus will not eat beef so lamb and chicken are popular. Many of the traditional methods would work with beef or pork, so feel free to try them if you don't share those religious beliefs. Many Hindus are strict vegetarians so meatless dishes are always available at Indian restaurants, and very good they are too. The curry is an excellent way of making vegetables interesting. Another influence of the Moslem faith is complete abstention from alcohol so it's never used in cooking or served with meals. Apparently this was difficult for the early Persians who had a great tradition of wine making and used it extensively in their cooking before they converted to Islam.

Dairy products such as milk, cream and cheese are used very little, if at all. This is probably because many adults cannot digest the particular sugar, called lactose, which is found in milk. This 'lactose intolerance' is common in people who are not of white-skinned, European origin. It's very rare among infants but usually occurs later in life. Where cheese is used it's usually the white crumbly sort like the Greek Feta. Meals are usually ended with fruit rather than made up deserts but the Persians, and to an even greater extent the Turks, do have a sweet tooth. Baklava is a typical sweet dish, made with flaky pastry with crushed nuts and, most importantly, drowned in sugar syrup. These concoctions are eaten at any time but especially in the mid afternoon. Because of the lactose intolerance sweet milky dishes like English style rice pudding or custard are never served.

Yoghurt is often used as an alternative to milk as it's sort of pre-digested and doesn't cause intolerance. Yoghurt thinned with water or fruit juice is a common drink especially among Moslems who don't drink alcohol. Cucumber and mint in yoghurt is called Tszadiki and is common in Greece and Turkey. Yoghurt is also used as the basis for the marinades for many tandoori dishes, especially 'Tikka'.

The Persians categorised their food into 'Hot' and 'Cold'. This has nothing to do with temperature and doesn't relate very well with our idea of spicy and bland foods but it's an important part of Persian cooking. They recognised that what you eat is important for your health and believed that a proper balance of hot and cold was essential for well being. A healthy, happy person would eat a balanced mixture of hot and cold foods while various diseases were considered to be either hot or cold in nature. A 'hot' disease would be cured by eating 'cold' food, and vice versa. The Chinese came to use a very similar system with the concept of 'Ying' and 'Yang'. The Chinese and Persian systems developed quite independently, and are different in detail, but there are so many similarities that the Persian traders, who came to China for the spice trade, were very comfortable with the Chinese concepts.

While the Persians took their food very seriously, the Turks almost made it into a religion. The Dervishes, apart from whirling to get themselves into a religious trance, ran the grand kitchens like monasteries. They had rules and rituals for everything and there was a strict hierarchy amongst the staff. This seemed to work very well and could have been the model for the extreme discipline of the French kitchen. When the power of the Turkish aristocracy collapsed, these experienced cooks – with their well trained staff – were out of work so they set up restaurants and this is why there are so many Turkish restaurants today.

The Centre Of The Universe

Civilisation really got going in Egypt, followed by Greece and then Rome, and they all border on the Mediterranean Sea. The word Mediterranean means 'Middle of the World' and, as far as they were concerned, the world was the middle of the universe. A lot of countries have Mediterranean coastlines and they all share certain characteristics in their cooking which isn't surprising because they share a similar climate and the same fish in the sea. The countries of the Mediterranean have been culturally linked for thousands of years by the traders who travelled around the sea and they would have passed on any good food ideas. The regional styles of cooking blend at the edges so Turkish and Greek cuisine is a mixture of Persian and Mediterranean, Morocco has an African influence and so on.

The typical flavour ingredients of Mediterranean cooking are olive oil, garlic, onion, tomato, lemon, basil and oregano. Meat is used in small amounts and a lot of fish is eaten on or near the coasts. Carbohydrate is eaten in the form of bread, pasta, rice or couscous, with one or other of these predominating in each region. Bread is popular in most of the countries but rice is important in Spain, couscous in Morocco and pasta in southern Italy. A salad of tomato, lettuce, or whatever's around, is eaten at most meals but cooked root vegetables aren't so common. Herbs and vegetables are usually used fresh but some vegetables such as olives, tomatoes, mushrooms, artichokes and beans are preserved in oil and eaten as appetizers, as in the Italian antipasto.

The Italian style of cooking is well known around the world from the many Italian restaurants. These restaurants are not so much influenced by a history of aristocrats and palaces so the food is more like a family would eat at home. In a simple Italian restaurant the choice is pizza or pasta. A pizza is a large, cooked open sandwich. The base is bread and the topping usually includes tomato and cheese with just about anything else added. Pizza is unusual in that it's one of the few popular dishes that relies on cooked cheese. Basil and oregano are invariably used for flavouring and black pepper is put on at the table.

Pasta is the same as noodles, in fact the similarity is so great that it's likely that the idea was brought to Italy from China by the Persian spice merchants but, just to confuse things, the word noodle is German. The Italians have a multitude of shapes for pasta but they're all made of the same stuff, durum wheat. The Italian pasta that is most like the Chinese noodles is vermicelli (which means little worms). Spaghetti is also long and round but fatter than vermicelli. Macaroni is fatter still, with a hole down the middle, and it's cut into short lengths. Gnocchi are shell shaped and fusilli are like corkscrews. There are lots more shapes and many of the shapes have different names depending on who you ask. The main reason for all these shapes, apart from showing off, is that they work best with different consistencies of sauce. A smooth pasta like spaghetti needs a thin sauce that will coat it easily but complicated shapes are best with a thick, heavy, chunky sauce that will get trapped in all the little corners. The finer noodles are put into soup just like in the far east.

Most of the sauces don't rely on meat, either there isn't any at all or there's just a little for taste. The favourite English 'Bolognese' sauce isn't known in Italy but it's based on a meat sauce from Bologna. Pasta sauces usually have some olive oil and either tomatoes or basil or both. Garlic and onion usually get in there as well and hard cheeses such as Parmesan and Pecorino are used for thickening. Cream is sometimes used for thickening but it's not so common. Pesto is a sauce made from basil and cheese and it's used extensively in Italian cooking.

I've experimented with Italian style cooking and I've come up with some interesting and easy dishes. I use a mixture of vegetables preserved in oil as the basis for a quick pasta sauce. These vegetables are found in most supermarkets nowadays and may be labelled 'Antipasto'. Just chop up whatever you fancy into small pieces, mix together and add to your pasta. Don't worry about the oil covering the vegetables, you need some of that to help the pasta slip down. You can add basil and oregano and stuff if you want. I also use ready made pesto from a jar and I perk it up with English mustard, ginger and garlic purée. Like that it makes a pasta sauce by itself or a good dip for crisps or tortilla chips.

Spain has had a major influence on the way the world eats, by an indirect route. The Spanish were the first to colonise America and settled in Mexico and the area that became the southern states. Their style of cooking mixed with the native Mexican style and gave rise to the typical Tex-Mex (Texas-Mexico) style that we know today. Corn grows there better than wheat so we see corn bread, polenta, tortillas and tacos. These are made in a similar way to wheat bread but they don't rise in the same way (no gluten – no bubbles). Chilli is an important flavour ingredient and most Mexican food has some in it. Typical chilli dishes are the famous Chilli con Carne (which translates as chilli and meat and consists of minced meat and beans in a sauce with a lot of chilli) and Salsa (a salad of tomato, onion and chilli).

Rice is used in both Spain and Italy but it's usually cooked with pieces of meat and vegetables to make a complete meal on its own; in Spain it's called Paella and in Italy it's Risotto and they both have similarities with the Persian Pilau rice. Paella in particular has the delicacy and subtlety typical of Persian cooking in its use of the flavour and colour of saffron. The Italians make a dumpling of rice with a meat and tomato sauce which is very like the Persian and Turkish dumplings. It's called Arancini, which means orange, because it looks like one, not because it tastes like one.

Morocco is a cultural mixture of African, Spanish and Moslem influences which gives it a style of its own. The main carbohydrate is couscous which is best with a thin, wet sauce; chicken stewed in a lemony soup is a typical accompaniment. The Moroccans have a particular liking for sweet sauces with meat.

Everything But The Squeal
The food of northern Europe has never been fashionable but its influence on what people really eat, as opposed to what they feel they should eat, has always been very strong. The main characteristic that distinguishes the cooking of northern Europe is being able to survive through the winter. This isn't a problem in Mediterranean or tropical countries where there's always something fresh to eat. Obviously, with modern methods of distributing and transporting food, living through the unproductive times of the year is no longer a problem but the historical influence is very strong.

To get through the winter you need a source of carbohydrate for energy to keep you warm and this was provided by bread and vegetables. Bread doesn't keep for very long and wheat is only harvested in the summer but, fortunately, flour keeps quite well. The vegetables were those that can be harvested through the winter, like brussels sprouts, kale, leeks, parsnips, spinach, swedes and turnips, or vegetables that can be stored such as beetroot, cabbages, carrots, onions, potatoes and radish. We can still see this in the traditional English Christmas dinner which always includes parsnips and brussels sprouts. Before potatoes came into Europe the other root vegetables would have been much more important. For example, parsnips were a major part of the diet in England, as turnips were in Scotland.

Another way to store vegetables is to dry them. Beans, peas and lentils can be dried quite easily by hanging them up indoors in their pods. Beans treated this way are called haricots. Dried peas were eaten as pease pudding and reconstituted dried beans were used in stews and soups. Vegetables were preserved as pickles, with onions being the favourite in England, while sauerkraut (cabbage pickled in salt) was an important part of the German winter diet. Some fruit, such as apples, could be kept but most was preserved as jam or chutney.

Near sea coasts, lakes and rivers, fish was an important source of fat and protein. Fish is famous for its lack of keeping ability and northern Europe came up with various preserving methods to deal with this. Most of the techniques work best on oily fish so herring is the most common, closely followed by mackerel. Herring is smoked: kippers, bloaters and buckling are all herrings smoked to different degrees. Herring is pickled: rollmop and bismark are well known names but there are many varieties of pickled herring in Scandinavia (in fact they just about live on pickled herring even today). Herring is salted: it can either be dried out completely or allowed to turn to jelly, as in the Maatjes herring. Of course, the king of smoked fish is salmon which, although a luxury food, is commonly available – especially in Scandinavia where the Norwegians make Gravad Laks which is smoked salmon with dill. This is presumably why New Yorkers call smoked salmon 'Lox'. (When your friends get funny about the Japanese eating raw fish remind them that smoked salmon is also eaten raw.)

Haddock and mackerel are usually found lightly smoked. Smoked haddock is a favourite in Scotland where small ones are called Arbroath Smokies and it's also the traditional fish in kedgeree. Kedgeree is a dish based freely on an Indian dish of the same name and offered as part of the Victorian breakfast, a terrifyingly large meal by today's standards. Think of it as the English equivalent of Paella or Risotto – a mixture of rice, fish, and hard boiled egg, with a certain amount of curry spice. I make my own version of kedgeree, not for breakfast but for dinner. I prefer to use smoked mackerel and I get the type with black peppercorns on it which can give enough spiciness on its own but I usually cook the rice with some curry paste in the water for more taste.

Most farmers kept a few animals such as cows, chickens and pigs. The cows and chickens were worth looking after carefully as they would give a continuous supply of milk and eggs as well as occasionally supplying more cows and chickens and, as a bonus, would supply meat at the end of their productive lives. The pigs would eat anything the chickens, cows and people didn't eat and would ultimately be eaten themselves. The nutritional value of meat was well understood even before the word nutrition was invented and every bit of an animal was used, nothing was wasted. In fact, in Yorkshire they say they use every part of a pig but its squeal! Everything means blood, bones, guts, skin and hooves as well as the meat, offal and fat.

Blood, especially pig's blood, is used to make black pudding which is found in northern England, Scotland, the north of France and Germany. The bones were not eaten but used as fertilizer or to make glue. The guts were eaten as tripe or used to make sausage casings and condoms (there were a lot more sausages than condoms because the condoms weren't very good and hardly anyone used them). The skin was made into leather and the hooves were used to make jelly and oil; the most productive hooves seem to be those of young cattle (calves foot jelly and neat's foot oil).

The meat was preserved by curing and smoking and sometimes drying. The pig was such an important part of the diet that there are special names for preserved pig meat: bacon and ham. All the bits of meat and fat that were left over after the carcase had been butchered were made into sausages and pies. Some of the sausages were also preserved by the same methods as the meat. Sausages and other made-up meat dishes are a major part of northern European cooking. These days they are especially popular for light lunches and snacks and are part of the enormous fast food industry.

Fast food is a German invention. No one in the other European countries would have dreamt of hurrying a meal but apparently the Germans were quite keen to get their food quickly, eat it and be gone. This wouldn't have had much impact on the world except that many of the emigrants to North America were German and their way of eating became popular. It's them we have to thank for the hamburger (from Hamburg, there's no ham in it) and the hot dog with a frankfurter (from Frankfurt) or a weinerwurst or weenie (from Vienna – I know that's in Austria but it's close). The first hamburgers were served in toasted bread cut from a loaf rather than in a bun and you might like to try this at home. If you want to make hot dogs at home try this trick from the back of a sausage packet I saw in America: put the sausage in the bun and wrap the lot in a paper kitchen towel. Heat this in the microwave for about a minute. You'll find it's cooked through, the meat juices have soaked into the bun, the microwave is clean because the paper stopped any liquid from getting out and the paper holds the sandwich together. I also think the sausage cooks quicker this way because of the heat insulation provided by the bread.

Just as the influence of the southern United States spread the style of Spanish and Mexican cooking around the world, the cultural colonialism of the northern States spread the cooking of northern Europe, including northern Italy. So now hot dogs, hamburgers and pizzas are found all around the world and it can be quite difficult to find the original local cuisine. The other kinds of sausage and the meat pies that you find in northern Europe didn't become popular in the USA so they haven't been spread around the world in the same way. If they had we could have had Ronald Ramsbottom and the University of Porkpieology or maybe Pie and Mash Hut.

The favourite foods of one region can seem quite revolting to another. Jellied eels were – and still are – very popular in southern England, especially around London. A lot of people are upset by the mere idea of a black pudding and retch at the thought of what goes into a haggis. (These people are a lost cause and tend not to come to my dinner parties.) Yorkshire wouldn't be Yorkshire without tripe and onions, and tripe sausages (Andouille) are a favourite in Normandy but there are still many people who turn up their noses at these non exotic dishes.

Milk is preserved by turning it into butter, cream and cheese and these dairy products are a very important part of the northern European diet. Lactose intolerance is uncommon among northern European people so adults are quite happy to drink cow's milk and eat cream and cheese. The milky dessert is an English favourite with examples such as rice pudding, semolina and tapioca. In fact, up until quite recently, most rice in England was eaten as rice pudding. Cheese is traditionally eaten, with biscuits, as a separate course of the meal but it also turns up in all sorts of savoury snacks and light meals such as the famous ploughman's lunch.

Wok's Up Doc?

The biggest influences on Far Eastern cookery are the wok and chopsticks. The wok, in case you don't know, is a large deep frying pan with a curved bottom. It was born out of the necessity of making the best use of a small amount of poor fuel. The Far East isn't blessed with the extensive forest and coal deposits of northern Europe and has to make do with a small amount of fast burning wood. The wok is made of relatively thin metal so it heats up fast and it's large so it can get all the heat out of a fierce, fast burning fire. Such a fire can't be kept going long so a very fast method of cooking, known as stir frying, was invented. In stir frying a small amount of oil is used and it's made very hot. The ingredients are all cut small and placed to hand in the right quantities. They are thrown into the wok and tossed around with abandon (at this point I'm tempted to say they do it again with a band off but it's a terrible joke so I won't). Speed is of the essence: the small pieces of food cook very quickly, in a matter of seconds, and if left any longer they'll burn.

The small pieces of food suit the chopsticks which can't cope with large chunks of food unless it's soft enough to be pulled apart. The cook has to cut up all the food into bite size portions as there will be no knives at the table. The ancient feudal regimes of the Far East were so repressive that only the lords and their guards were permitted to carry anything which might be used as a weapon. This is why they ate with wooden sticks and also why they invented devastating fighting techniques using only their bare hands or apparently harmless agricultural tools.

In most of the Far East, rice is the main food and is the focal point of all proper meals. The dishes that accompany the rice are strongly flavoured and served in quite small portions but there may be a lot of different ones. Small amounts of meat are used, if any is available, but it has to be the best quality and it's usually cooked with vegetables. There's very little good farming land in Japan and most of it is used for growing rice so there's hardly any dairy or beef farming. When cattle are raised for meat great care is taken that they produce the best beef.

I was once told a story about the famous beef from the Kobe region by a Japanese tour guide. This guide looked like the plump, smiling statues of Buddha that you see everywhere and he obviously liked his food. He told us that we were travelling through Kobe where the local farmers would keep one animal for beef production and look after it as if it were one of the family, or better. To get the best beef the farmer would feed the animal on beer and massage it every day. Our guide said that, although the beef was superb, he'd rather eat hamburgers and have the beer and massage himself!

A lot of fish is eaten in the Far East and the Japanese, in particular, are known for their love of raw fish which has to be very fresh. A Japanese chef will reject a fish if it isn't wriggling strongly enough! The raw fish is made into sushi and sushimi which are various bite size nibbles in which the fish is combined with rice and seaweed. These are eaten in bars as snacks rather than as a main meal. Historically it's been so difficult for the Japanese to get enough protein that they've made the best of every source available. This has led them to the use of the soya bean.

Soya beans are very nutritious, being mostly protein and fat with very little starch (other beans are mostly starch) but they have hardly any taste so you wouldn't want to eat a plate of them on their own. Soya is used to make various products which are an important part of the Japanese diet. A kind of milk can be extracted from the plant and this can be used as a substitute for dairy milk; and a curd called 'Tofu', which is similar to cheese, is made from it in large quantities. Tofu is a major source of protein and much of Japanese cookery is devoted to making it taste of something. The beans are fermented to make soy sauce, which is a highly flavoured liquid used in place of salt, and miso, which is a similar product in paste form. Apart from soy sauce, the main flavouring ingredients in Japanese cookery are garlic, ginger and onion.

I explained earlier that I've noticed a trend of dishes becoming hotter as you get nearer the equator, well it's most noticeable in the Far East. Indonesia is on the equator and is the source of most of the herbs and spices that were traded around the world, at first by land on the spice road via China, India, Iran and Turkey and later carried by sea by Portuguese merchants. Turmeric, galangal, ginger, lemon grass, tamarind, nutmeg, basil, mint and cloves are all native and they're used fresh in the local cooking. These herbs and spices can also be grown in Vietnam where they are used fresh in large quantities. In Thailand the food is very hot and chillies are eaten at every meal, including breakfast. The Thais like variety and experiment with mixtures such as vegetables cooked with meat and fruit mixed with savories. In the south of China the cuisine is based on rice and is similar to that found in the other southern countries. Hong Kong and Canton are in the south of China and most of the Chinese restaurants around the world are run by people from this area so our knowledge of Chinese food is mostly of the Cantonese style.

Japanese food isn't hot or spicy. The flavouring mainly comes from soy sauce, from rice wine (both the dry type called Sake and the sweet called Mirin), from citrus fruit, and from Dashi which is flakes of dried Bonito (a large fish of the Tuna family). Korea is at the same latitude as Japan but it's on the mainland of Asia so the climate is more extreme with hotter summers and colder winters. The most important ingredient of Korean cooking is Kimchee which is cabbage, with lots of garlic and other strong flavoured spices and vegetables, pickled in salt. Most people make their own Kimchee and everyone has their own recipes so no two batches are the same.

Meals which aren't based on rice consist of noodles, usually in soup. This is the everyday lunch in most of the Far East. (It may surprise English readers to know that instant pot noodles in the Far East are really very good. They're not to be confused with the version we usually get here which has a sticky consistency and far too much salt and monosodium glutamate for my liking. If you can find genuine pot noodles from the Far East give them a try.) Noodles are made from rice or wheat, the rice ones being lighter in colour. Obviously rice noodles are more common in rice growing areas or where it isn't practical to grow wheat.

There are many different types of noodles but the shapes aren't as fancy as the Italian ones, probably because soft wheat is used and they wouldn't hold the shape. Wheat is a relatively new introduction into the Far East (before that millet was used) so there isn't a tradition of making bread and most of the wheat is used for noodles. Further north, wheat becomes as important as rice and it's mostly eaten as noodles and steamed dumplings.

Steaming is a major method of cooking in the Far East. Rice is usually steamed and many ingredients can be steamed at the same time by stacking them up on top of each other in bamboo baskets. Ovens are rare, which is another reason why bread hasn't caught on. The reason such a fuss is made about Peking duck is that the duck is roasted in an oven. This is no big deal in the West but in ancient China an oven would have been made specially just for this meal. The high point of the meal is the roast skin which is eaten in little pancakes with spring onions, traditionally assembled at the table by the guests. Every bit of the duck is used, the meat is used in a stir fry dish and the carcase is used to make soup.

Out Of Africa

Africa is a huge continent that has had hardly any impact on cooking outside its boundaries. There's no restaurant tradition and most of the people around the world who originated in Africa were taken as slaves and denied their own culture. The Caribbean islands have generated a culture in which the African is mixed with Spanish and southern USA influences. This is reflected in the food of the area and is also found in the places that these people emigrated to, including England.

The carbohydrate in the African diet is provided by plantains, which are green bananas, and various roots and tubers such as yams, sweet potatoes and cassava roots. Yams and sweet potatoes can be prepared like ordinary potatoes but cassava needs a lot of work to make it edible. Spicy stews and soups are eaten with the vegetables, the main spice being chilli powder.

Africa is known for its variety of wildlife and the native rural people eat anything they can catch. However, the people who have moved to the towns want to eat like the Europeans who used to be their masters and this means cattle for beef and wheat for bread. Unfortunately neither of these do very well in Africa: it's either too wet or too dry for wheat and the tsetse fly causes serious disease in cattle. The cultivation of wheat probably started in Egypt but that was only in the limited area irrigated by the Nile. The native animals are resistant to tsetse fly but the new middle class won't eat 'Bush Meat' because it's peasant food. The native plants and animals can survive the difficult weather conditions (mostly drought) and the diseases but they don't have the same high yields as the introduced rice, wheat and cattle. The people have exchanged a small but dependable food supply for a potentially higher yield which fails completely if conditions aren't right. This is part of the reason for the famines that we hear of in Africa.

10

EPILOGUE

If you've read and understood this book then you've either learnt a lot or you already knew a lot before you started. I've touched on most of what you're supposed to learn in school – physics, chemistry, history, geography and maybe even a little art – so if anyone asks why they have to learn all these things you've got an answer: it's so we can all be better cooks!

Bon Appetit.

INDEX

Index

RIGHT WAY
PUBLISHING POLICY

HOW WE SELECT TITLES

RIGHT WAY consider carefully every deserving manuscript. Where an author is an authority on his subject but an inexperienced writer, we provide first-class editorial help. The standards we set make sure that every **RIGHT WAY** book is practical, easy to understand, concise, informative and delightful to read. Our specialist artists are skilled at creating simple illustrations which augment the text wherever necessary.

CONSISTENT QUALITY

At every reprint our books are updated where appropriate, giving our authors the opportunity to include new information.

FAST DELIVERY

We sell **RIGHT WAY** books to the best bookshops throughout the world. It may be that your bookseller has run out of stock of a particular title. If so, he can order more from us at any time – we have a fine reputation for "same day" despatch, and we supply any order, however small (even a single copy), to any bookseller who has an account with us. We prefer you to buy from your bookseller, as this reminds him of the strong underlying public demand for **RIGHT WAY** books. Readers who live in remote places, or who are housebound, or whose local bookseller is unco-operative, can order direct from us by post.

FREE

If you would like an up-to-date list of all **RIGHT WAY** titles currently available, please send a stamped self-addressed envelope to

ELLIOT RIGHT WAY BOOKS,
LOWER KINGSWOOD, TADWORTH,
SURREY, KT20 6TD, U.K.